Honey Pie

AMIGURUMI DRESS-UP DOLL
WITH PICNIC PLAY SET

Honey Pie

AMIGURUMI DRESS-UP DOLL WITH PICNIC PLAY SET

CROCHET PATTERNS FOR 12" DOLL plus DOLL CLOTHES, PICNIC BLANKET, BARBECUE PLAYMAT & ACCESSORIES

Linda Wright

Dedicated to my dear friend, Anna

Also by Linda Wright

Amigurumi Christmas Ornaments
Amigurumi Golf Club Covers
Honey Bunny Amigurumi Dress Up Doll
Amigurumi Animal Hats
Amigurumi Animal Hats Growing Up
Amigurumi Animal Hats for 18-Inch Dolls
Amigurumi Holiday Hats for 18-Inch Dolls
Amigurumi Toilet Paper Covers
Toilet Paper Origami
Toilet Paper Origami On a Roll

Credits

Photography: Randy and Linda Wright
Illustrations on Pages 1 and 77: Jess Perna

All rights reserved. Permission is granted to copy or reprint portions for any noncommercial use, except they may not be posted online without permission. You may sell the finished products that you make yourself at your local bazaar, craft fair, etc. but not on the internet. Items cannot be mass produced without the publisher's written permission. Contact the publisher with licensing inquiries.

Copyright © 2020 Linda Wright
Edition 1.1

Lindaloo Enterprises
P.O. Box 90135
Santa Barbara, California 93190
United States
sales@lindaloo.com

ISBN: 978-1-937564-14-8
Library of Congress Control Number: 2019919237

CONTENTS

GETTING STARTED

Introduction 7
Supplies 8
Abbreviations 9
Gauge 9
How to Read a Pattern 9

DOLL

Honey Pie 12

WARDROBE

Dresses
Wildflower Dress 16
Birdie Dress 18

Tops
Basic Blouse 19
Daisy Top 20
Jacket 22
Honey Bear Blouse 24

Bottoms
Drawstring Shorts 25
Butterfly Jeans 26
Fancy Pants 26
Button-Front Skirt 27
Simple Skirt 27

Footwear
Espadrilles 28
Ballet Flats 28
Sandals 29

Accessories
Bow Barrette 30
Flower Barrette 30
Watermelon Purse 31
Tote Bag 32
Barbecue Apron 33

Nightwear
Night Gown 34

BED

Slice-of-Pie Sleeping Bag 35

PICNIC

Picnic Blanket	36
Barbecue Pit Play Mat	38
Picnic Basket	39

Food

Cheeseburger	41
Chicken Drumstick	42
Corn on the Cob	43
Watermelon Slice	44
Fruit Drink	45
S'mores	46
Blueberry Pie	47
Ketchup & Mustard	50
Potato Chips	51
Hot Dog	52
Vegetable Kebab	53

Accessories

Spatula	54
Picnic Plates	55

Picnic Game

Mini FrizzBee	56

Friends

Honey Bear	57
Honey Ant	59
Honey Bee	62

BASICS

Stitches	64
Techniques	66
Templates	69
Resources	73
Yarn	73

BONUS

Honey Pie Coloring Page	77
Honey Pie Recipe	79

INTRODUCTION

Meet Honey Pie — an adorable doll with honey-colored curls who loves picnics. In this book, you will find crochet patterns for a complete picnic play set including Honey Pie's pals: Honey Bear, Honey Bee and Honey Ant. Those three are always hungry and ready to picnic!

The patterns in Honey Pie's book include a checked Picnic Blanket that is big enough for all 4 dolls to spread out and eat, a Picnic Basket and a Barbecue Pit Play Mat. Children can have fun cooking amigurumi food on the BBQ Pit—even toasting little marshmallows for S'mores.

A wardrobe of cute doll clothes has been provided. By using different color combinations and decorative embellishments, you can make myriad creations. When you dress your doll, remember that the clothes are designed to slide on feet-first. For bedtime, the Slice-of-Pie Sleeping Bag will keep your doll warm as pie.

Before starting, be sure to read through the next two introductory pages plus the Stitches and Techniques sections at the back of the book. You will find some helpful tips. If you're new to crocheting and like to learn by watching, YouTube.com offers a treasure trove of excellent crocheting tutorials. These are also great for experienced crocheters who need to brush up. I have assembled a collection of my favorite videos on Pinterest. You can view them at www.pinterest.com/LindalooEnt/ on a board named "Amigurumi Tutorials".

If you want to make a doll that can hold a pose, wire can be added inside the arms, legs or both. (See "Adding Wire" on page 68.) Don't be intimidated at the thought...it's not difficult. Using pipe cleaners for soft but posable limbs is a fun way to make your amigurumi characters more dynamic. Other techniques I'm excited to share in this book include:

- how to make a cardboard structure for the Picnic Basket
- how to stiffen yarn for the Graham Crackers
- how to crochet comical movable mouths for Honey Bee and Honey Ant
- how to make a fun and functional Spatula
- how to make Honey Pie's fabulous curls.

This book uses U.S. crochet terms. If an instruction says sc, that is a U.S. single crochet—or a U.K. double crochet. Please refer to the stitch diagrams at the back of the book to be sure you are making the stitches as intended.

Honey Pie is the follow-up to my previous book, *Honey Bunny Amigurumi Dress-Up Doll with Garden Play Mat*. Together with Honey Pie, the two dolls are similar enough in size to be perfect playmates. They can share accessories and many of their clothes. Honey Pie's legs are longer, so in the case of pants, adjustments would have to be made.

I hope you and the little ones in your life have fun with my designs. If you enjoy my book, please consider leaving a review at your online place of purchase. Other customers would appreciate it too! Although this is an amigurumi book, I couldn't resist including two little extras, so I also hope you will try your hand at the Honey Pie coloring page and my recipe for a yummy Honey Pie!

♥ Linda

Supplies

Yarn

These projects have been made with acrylic yarns that are readily available and inexpensive. Worsted-weight yarn is used for items that need a sturdy structure. DK/Light Worsted is used for items that have a more delicate nature or that need to drape. Check each pattern for its yarn weight specification. I used various yarn brands from my stash to make these little items. They are listed in the Resources section at the back of the book.

Crochet Hook

The following hooks are used: E4/3.5mm, F5/3.75mm, G6/4mm and H8/5mm. My favorite hook is the Clover Soft Touch. I love the thick handle and the shape of the head which inserts easily into a stitch.

Yarn Needle

You will need a large-eyed needle to sew the various pieces of your items together and also to finish them off by weaving the loose ends into your work. Yarn needles with a blunt point are readily available but I frequently like to use a one with a sharp point. These can be hard to find in stores, so if you'd like one, plan to shop online. My favorite is the Size 14 Chenille or Embroidery needle.

Stitch Markers

Stitch markers are used to keep track of where a round or row of crochet begins and ends. You can use a bobby pin, safety pin or purchased stitch markers. You can also use a scrap of yarn (see page 67). Making the correct number of stitches is important, so count to double check if ever you're not sure.

Safety Eyes

Plastic safety eyes give amigurumi a professional look. Each eye has a post section and a washer. To attach, work post into a gap between stitches. Place washer against post, lay eye against a hard surface and press washer firmly. A socket wrench or the tube portion of an old pen can be helpful for pushing the washer down.

Safety eyes, or animal eyes, frequently include a warning such as "Contains small parts that may present a choking hazard for children under 3". If the doll is for a child under age 3, embroidery or small felt circles can be used as alternatives to plastic eyes.

Straight Pins

Use standard dressmaker's pins or long corsage pins to hold pieces in place before sewing.

Ruler

For measuring and marking.

Sewing Needle & Thread

You will need these sewing box basics. If you don't have a supply of thread, one spool of clear nylon thread, called "invisible thread", will match everything.

Row Counter

Well worth the investment, a row counter keeps track of what round or row of the pattern you are crocheting. A pencil and paper can also be used. Crochet apps for mobile devices are available too. A simple Android app that I like is called Minimalist Stitch Counter.

Removable Notes

Use small sticky notes to keep track of your place in a pattern. Every time you complete a round or a row, move the note down to reveal the next line of instructions. I wouldn't work without one!

Scissors

You will need a small pair of sharp scissors.

Stuffing

Polyester fiberfill is the best stuffing material. Yarn scraps can be used for stuffing small pieces. The eraser end of a new pencil, a blunt-tipped chopstick or 6-inch straight-tip serrated tweezers make great stuffing tools. I especially love my tweezers for small pieces. Using them, I can easily insert a wad of stuffing through a tiny opening.

Abbreviations

The following abbreviations are used:

yd = yard

st = stitch

ch = chain

sc = single crochet

hdc = half double crochet

dc = double crochet

sl st = slip stitch

rnd = round

sc2tog = single crochet 2 stitches together

sc3tog = single crochet 3 stitches together

dc2tog = double crochet 2 stitches together

sp = space

yo = yarn over

* * = a set of stitches

( ) = stitch count; also indicates a group of sts worked together in the same stitch or space

Gauge

Gauge is a measure of how big your stitches are. It's very common for gauge to vary from person to person because not all crocheters stitch the same way. Yarn selection also affects gauge. Some yarns are thinner than others despite being in the same weight category. To alter your gauge, adjust your crochet tension (tightness); change to a larger or smaller crochet hook; try a different brand of hook; or try a different brand of yarn. The following gauge is used in these patterns.

With **G6/4mm hook** and **DK, Light Worsted yarn**:

20 sc = 4"

25 rows = 4"

With **G6/4mm hook** and **Worsted Weight yarn**:

18 sc = 4"

21 rows = 4"

How to Read a Pattern

Each round or row is written on a new line. Most rounds have a repeated section of instructions that are written between two asterisks *like this*. The instruction between the asterisks is to be repeated as many times as indicated before you move on to the next step. At the end of a round, the total number of stitches to be made in that round is indicated in parentheses (like this).

Let's look at a round from Honey Pie.

Rnd 6: *sc in next 4 sts, 2 sc in next st* 6 times (36 sts).

This means:

Rnd 6	This is the 6th round of the pattern.
sc in next 4 sts	Make 1 single crochet stitch in each of the next 4 stitches
2 sc in next st	Make 2 single crochet stitches, both in the same stitch
6 times	Repeat everything between * and * 6 times.
(36 sts)	The round will have a total of 36 stitches.

So, following the instructions for Round 6, you will:

single crochet in the next 4 sts, 2 sc in the next st,
single crochet in the next 4 sts, 2 sc in the next st,
single crochet in the next 4 sts, 2 sc in the next st,
single crochet in the next 4 sts, 2 sc in the next st,
single crochet in the next 4 sts, 2 sc in the next st,
single crochet in the next 4 sts, 2 sc in the next st,

for a total of 36 stitches.

Honey Pie

Honey Pie is made of worsted-weight yarn. This doll was made with beige skin and honey-colored hair but those features can be customized in any way you wish. See page 73 for the specific yarns used here.

Choose the yarn for your doll's hair carefully. Some yarns are better than others for curly hair. I suggest testing a yarn first by making a sample strand to make sure the curls are to your liking. My favorite is a thick brand of worsted. I like the loft and firmness which give the hair nice body and bounce.

The doll parts are crocheted as continuous spirals by working in the round. When crocheting small cylinders such as the arms and legs, a running stitch marker is ideal (see page 67). The eraser end of a new pencil makes a great stuffing tool: by twisting the pencil as you push, the eraser will grab the stuffing nicely. Underwear is created as part of the doll to eliminate the need for an extra layer of bulk under her clothing.

If you would like your doll to be able to hold a pose, wire can be added inside. Instructions for a full or partial armature are provided in the Techniques section at the back of the book. Without wire, Honey Pie will be soft and cuddly with hinges at the top of her legs so she can sit nicely on the picnic blanket.

SIZE

12" tall

SUPPLIES

G6/4mm crochet hook

100 yds of Worsted weight yarn in beige

115 yds of Worsted weight yarn in honey

Small amount of Worsted weight yarn in pink

Invisible sewing thread

2 black safety eyes, 10mm

Fabric glue (Fabri-Tac)

Stuffing

HEAD

Make a magic ring, ch 1.

Rnd 1: 6 sc in ring, pull ring closed tight (6 sts).

Rnd 2: 2 sc in each st around. Place marker for beginning of rnd and move marker up as each rnd is completed (12 sts).

Rnd 3: *sc in next st, 2 sc in next st* 6 times (18 sts).

Rnd 4: *sc in next 2 sts, 2 sc in next st* 6 times (24 sts).

Rnd 5: *sc in next 3 sts, 2 sc in next st* 6 times (30 sts).

Rnd 6: *sc in next 4 sts, 2 sc in next st* 6 times (36 sts).

Rnd 7: sc in each st around.

Rnd 8: *sc in next 5 sts, 2 sc in next st* 6 times (42 sts).

Rnds 9-13: sc in each st around.

Rnd 14: *sc in next 5 sts, sc2tog* 6 times (36 sts).

Rnd 15: *sc in next 4 sts, sc2tog* 6 times (30 sts).

Rnd 16: *sc in next 3 sts, sc2tog* 6 times (24 sts).

Rnd 17: *sc in next 2 sts, sc2tog* 6 times (18 sts).

Rnd 18: *sc in next st, sc2tog* 6 times (12 sts).

Sl st in next st. Fasten off.

Stuff head half way, attach eyes between Rnds 12-13 with an interspace of 9 sts; or, eyes may be glued in later if desired. Finish stuffing head firmly: push stuffing against edges of head to fill out the shape of the sphere.

For **nose**, embroider 2 or 3 small sts and hide yarn tails inside head.

BODY

With pink yarn, make a magic ring, ch 1.

Rnd 1: 8 sc in ring, pull ring closed tight (8 sts).

Rnd 2: *sc in next st, 2 sc in next st* 4 times. Place marker for beginning of rnd and move marker up as each rnd is completed (12 sts).

Rnd 3: *sc in next st, 2 sc in next st* 6 times (18 sts).

Rnd 4: *sc in next 2 sts, 2 sc in next st* 6 times (24 sts).

Rnds 5-7: sc in each st around; change to beige in last st.

Rnds 8-17: sc in each st around.

Rnd 18: *sc in next 2 sts, sc2tog* 6 times (18 sts).

Rnd 19: *sc in next st, sc2tog* 6 times (12 sts).

Sl st in next st. Fasten off.

Stuff body firmly. Sew head and body together, packing in more stuffing at the junction for neck support when seam is nearly closed.

LEGS (MAKE 2)

The legs are made from the top down.

Ch 10, join with sl st to first ch to make a ring using care not to twist the chain.

Rnds 1-20: sc in each ch or st around. Place marker for beginning of rnd and move marker up as each rnd is completed (10 sts).

Rnd 21: for **foot**, 2 sc in next st, 4 sc in next 2 sts, 2 sc in next st, sc in next 6 sts (18 sts).

Rnds 22-23: sc in each st around.

Rnd 24: sc2tog 9 times (9 sts).

Fasten off. To close hole, thread ending tail onto needle, weave needle in and out around post of each st and pull tight.

Stuff legs up to the last 1/2 inch and leave the remaining portion unstuffed.

Flatten one leg so that foot faces **forward**. For **hinge**, join at right corner and work thru all layers as follows: sc in first 3 sts, hdc in next st, dc in last st. Fasten off.

Flatten 2nd leg so that foot faces **backward**. For **hinge**, join at right corner and work thru all layers as follows: sc in first 3 sts, hdc in next st, dc in last st. Fasten off.

Weave in ends.

With invisible thread, sew legs to bottom of body.

ARMS (MAKE 2)

Make a magic ring, ch 1.

Rnd 1: 9 sc in ring, pull ring closed tight (9 sts).

Rnds 2-3: sc in each st around. Place marker for beginning of rnd and move marker up as each rnd is completed.

Rnd 4: sc2tog twice, sc in next 5 sts (7 sts).

Rnds 5-20: sc in each st around.

Sl st in next st. Fasten off. With eraser end of new pencil, push stuffing into hand only; do not stuff arm.

Sew an arm to each side, 1 rnd down from top of body.

HAIR

Honey Pie's hair is created as a wig that is attached to the doll's head with sewing and glue.

WIG BASE

Make a magic ring, ch 1.

Rnd 1: 7 sc in ring, pull ring closed tight (7 sts).

Rnd 2: 2 sc in each st around. Place marker for beginning of rnd and move marker up as each rnd is completed (14 sts).

Now work in rows. Note: A chain 1 at the beginning of a row is for turning your work and does not count as a stitch.

Row 3: ch 1, turn, *sc in next 2 sts, 2 sc in next st* 3 times (12 sts).

Row 4: ch 1, turn, *sc in next 3 sts, 2 sc in next st* 3 times (15 sts).

Row 5: ch 1, turn, *sc in next 4 sts, 2 sc in next st* 3 times (18 sts).

Row 6: ch 1, turn, *sc in next 5 sts, 2 sc in next st* 3 times (21 sts).

Rows 7-10: ch 1, turn, dc in each st across.

Row 11: ch 1, turn, *dc in next 5 sts, dc2tog* 3 times (18 sts).

Row 12: ch 1, turn, *dc in next st, dc2tog* 6 times (12 sts).

Fasten off.

Rows 4-6 are worked in **front loops** only (see white dots in Photo A). Join with sl st in first unworked st of wig base Rnd 2.

Row 4: ch 11, turn, sc in 2nd ch from hook and in each remaining ch across (10 sts).

Rows 5-6: sl st in next st, ch 11, turn, sc in 2nd ch from hook and in each remaining ch across (10 sts).

Sl st in next st. Fasten off. Weave in ends.

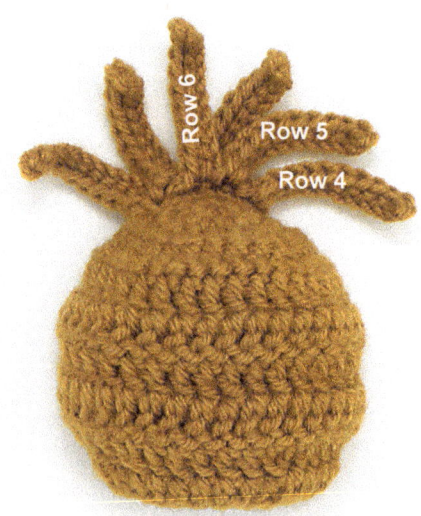

BANGS

Rows 1-3 are worked in **back loops** only (see blue dots in Photo A). Join with sl st in first unworked st of wig base Rnd 2 (see arrow in Photo A).

Row 1: sl st in next 2 sts, ch 11, turn, sc in 2nd ch from hook and in each remaining ch across (10 sts).

Rows 2-3: sl st in next st, ch 11, turn, sc in 2nd ch from hook and in each remaining ch across (10 sts).

Sl st in next st. Fasten off.

HAIR STRANDS (MAKE 34)

Chain 41.

Row 1: sc in 2nd ch from hook and in each remaining ch across (40 sts). Fasten off.

FINISHING

Turn wig base **wrong-side out** so that bangs will curve inward toward doll's head. Refer to white dots in photo below for placement of hair strands. Attach each strand by hooking its tails thru to inside of base and knotting the tails together. Tails of top 5 strands should straddle Rnd 1 and tails of remaining strands should straddle post of adjacent st. Trim knotted tails to 1/4".

Pin finished wig to doll so that Rnd 1 of wig base meets Rnd 1 of doll's head and bangs are at center front. Arrange bangs and pin in place. Lift bangs one-by-one, apply glue, lay back in position and replace pin until glue is dry.

Sew wig to head with running sts around edge of base.

Note: If you want more fullness in your doll's hair, make more hair strands and attach them where desired.

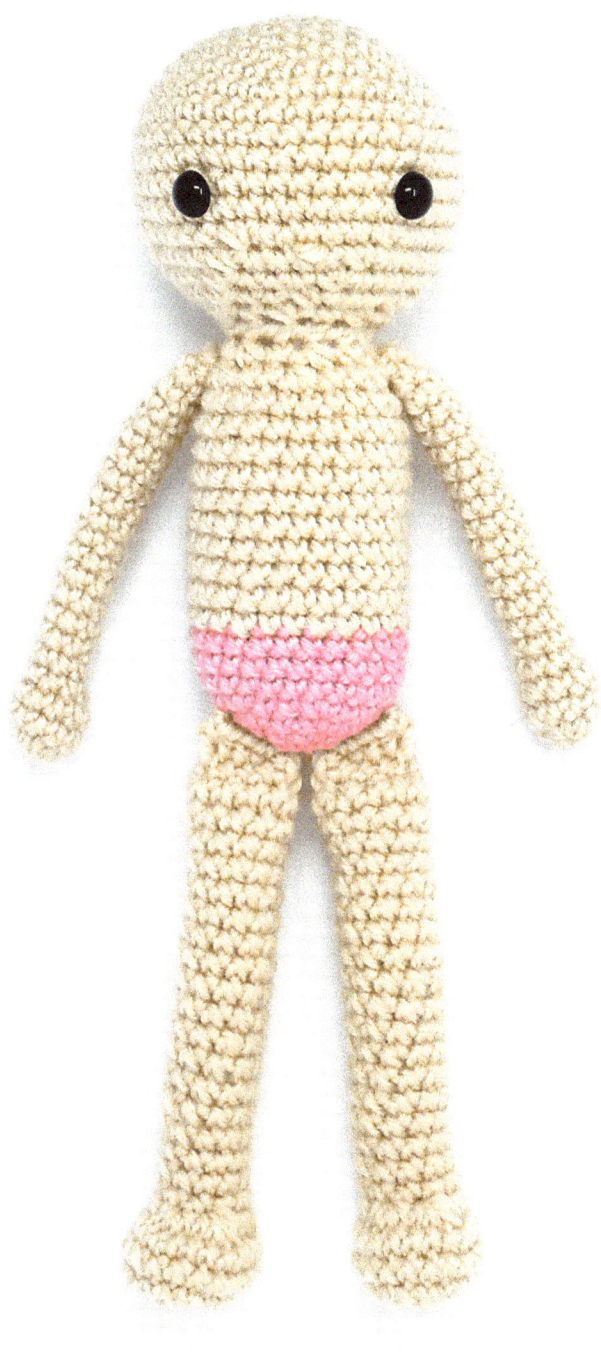

Wildflower Dress

The dress is made from the top down. The work is done back and forth in rows to the waistline. This creates an opening for buttons at the back. The skirt section is then made with joined rounds. Crocheted flowers add adornment.

SUPPLIES

E4/3.5mm and G6/4mm crochet hooks

80 yds of DK, Light Worsted yarn in lavender (dress)

Small amount of DK, Light Worsted yarn in assorted colors (flowers & vine)

3 buttons, 3/8"

Yellow beads, 4mm (optional)

Sewing thread

Note: A chain 1 at the beginning of a row is for turning your work and does not count as a stitch.

YOKE & BODICE

With G6/4mm crochet hook, ch 24.

Row 1: ch 1, turn, dc in each ch across (24 sts).

Row 2: ch 1, turn, *dc in next 2 sts, 2 dc in next st* across (32 sts).

Row 3: ch 1, turn, *dc in next 3 sts, 2 dc in next st* across (40 sts).

Row 4: ch 1, turn, *dc in next 4 sts, 2 dc in next st* across (48 sts).

Row 5: ch 1, turn, dc in next 6 sts; for **armhole**, ch 3, skip next 12 sts; dc in next 12 sts; for **armhole**, ch 3, skip next 12 sts; dc in next 6 sts (24 sts, 6 chs).

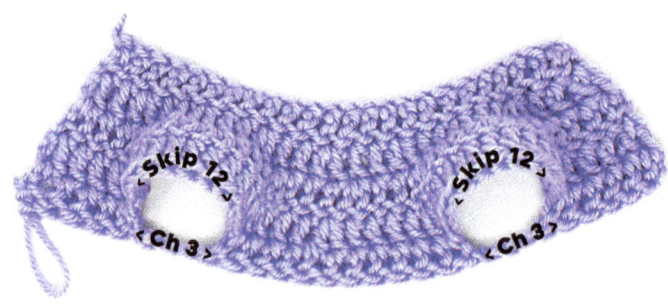

Row 6: ch 1, turn, dc in each st or ch across (30 sts).

Row 7: ch 1, turn, dc in each st across, join with sl st in first st.

SKIRT

Now work in joined rounds.

Rnd 8: ch 1, turn, 2 dc in each st around, join with sl st in first st (60 sts).

Rnd 9: ch 1, turn, *dc in next st, 2 dc next st* around, join with sl st in first st (90 sts).

Rnds 10-15: ch 1, turn, dc in each st around, join with sl st in first st.

Fasten off. Weave in ends.

FLOWER APPLIQUES (MAKE 9)

All sts except the chs are worked into the ring.

With E4/3.5mm crochet hook, make a magic ring, ch 1.

Rnd 1: *3 dc, sl st, ch 1* 5 times (5 petals).

Fasten off. Pull ring closed very tight and knot tails together.

LEAF APPLIQUES (MAKE 9)

The leaf is worked around a foundation chain.

With E4/3.5mm crochet hook, ch 4.

Rnd 1: sc in 2nd ch from hook, 2 hdc in next ch, sc in next ch; for **tip**, ch 2, sl st in 2nd ch from hook; sc in next ch, 2 hdc in next ch, sc in next ch. Join with sl st to first st.

Fasten off.

VINE

Make vine about 1" above hem of skirt. The vine is made with **surface sl st** as follows.

With G6/4mm crochet hook, hold yarn on wrong side of skirt.

Rnd 1: starting at center back, insert hook from right side to wrong side in space between sts, yarn over and pull up a loop (1 loop on hook), *insert hook from right side to wrong side in next space, yarn over and pull loop thru fabric and thru loop on hook* around. Fasten off.

Note: You will yarn over on the wrong side of the work and bring the loop thru to the right side of the work.

BELT

With G6/4mm crochet hook and green yarn, chain a string 18" long. Fasten off. Pull hard to tighten knots at each end. Trim tails to 1/2". Weave belt thru sts of Rnd 7. Tie in a bow at center front.

FINISHING

Sew buttons to one side of back opening. Use spaces between sts on opposite side for buttonholes.

Sew 1 flower to bodice and 8 flowers around vine at approximately 2" intervals. Sew a bead to center of each flower or embroider French Knots (see page 68).

Sew a leaf beside flower on bodice. Sew remaining leaves between flowers on vine as pictured. Weave in ends.

Birdie Dress

BIRD APPLIQUE

With E4/3.5mm crochet hook and red-orange yarn, make a magic ring, ch 1.

Rnd 1: for **head,** 10 dc in ring, pull ring closed tight, join with sl st in first st (10 sts).

Now work in rows for **body.**

Row 2: ch 2 (counts as dc), turn, dc in same st as where your ch started, 2 dc in next 2 sts (6 sts).

Row 3: ch 2 (counts as dc), turn, dc in same st as where your ch started, 2 dc in next 2 sts, hdc in next st, sc in next st (8 sts).

Row 4: turn (do not ch), sl st in next st, hdc in next st, dc in next st, 2 dc in next 3 sts (9 sts). Fasten off.

Beak: join yellow yarn to st at front of head, ch 2, sl st in same st. Fasten off.

Wing: with orange yarn, make a magic ring, ch 2. **Rnd 1:** 7 dc in ring, pull ring closed. Fasten off. Sew wing to body.

FLOWER APPLIQUE

With E4/3.5mm crochet hook and red-orange yarn, make a magic ring, ch 1.

Rnd 1: 5 sc in ring, pull ring closed tight, sl st in first st to join; change to yellow in last st (5 sts).

Rnd 2: (sl st, ch 2, 2 dc, ch 2, sl st) in each st around (5 petals). Fasten off. Knot tails together.

SUPPLIES

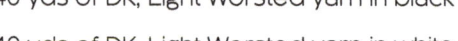

E4/3.5mm and G6/4mm crochet hooks

40 yds of DK, Light Worsted yarn in black

40 yds of DK, Light Worsted yarn in white

Small amount of DK, Light Worsted yarn in red-orange, orange and yellow

1 black bead, 4mm

3 buttons, 3/8"

Sewing thread

DRESS

Follow instructions for Wildflower Dress (see page 16), alternating black and white yarn for each row to make stripes. Make bird and flower appliques to sew on the front.

FINISHING

Sew bird to skirt section of dress. Sew bead to center of bird's head for eye. Sew flower to bodice of dress. Weave in ends.

Basic Blouse

Make 2

Sew   Sew

Sew   Sew

Two identical pieces are crocheted flat in rows and sewn together to make this easy top.

SUPPLIES

G6/4mm crochet hook

Small amount of DK, Light Worsted yarn

Note: A chain 1 at the beginning of a row is for turning your work and does not count as a stitch.

BLOUSE (MAKE 2)

Ch 18.

Rows 1-4: ch 1, turn, dc in each st across (18 sts).

Rows 5-7: ch 1, turn, dc in next 15 sts (15 sts).

Row 8: ch 4, turn, dc in 2nd ch from hook and each remaining ch or st across (18 sts).

Rows 9-11: ch 1, turn, dc in each st across (18 sts).

Fasten off.

FINISHING

Stack pieces and sew together across shoulders. Sew up sides leaving 1" open to make armholes. Weave in ends.

Basic Blouse Variation

Use multi-colored yarn for an easy elevated look.

Daisy Top

The Daisy Top is made from 2 daisy-motif granny squares that are worked in the round. If you've never made a granny square, you may want to visit YouTube for a granny square video tutorial to become familiar with the technique.

The daisy's petals are made from groups of dc that are abbreviated as 3dctog and 4dctog. See the next column for step-by-step instructions for these special stitches.

SUPPLIES

G6/4mm crochet hook

Small amount of DK, Light Worsted yarn in brown, yellow, light blue and dark blue

2 sew-on snap fasteners

Sewing thread

★ SPECIAL STITCHES USED IN THIS PATTERN

The abbreviations 3dctog and 4dctog mean 3 or 4 double crochet (dc) stitches that you gather on your hook and then pull yarn thru all of them at once to form a petal shape. They are very easy stitches to master.

3DCTOG (STARTING CLUSTER): Yo, insert hook in indicated st, yo and pull up a loop, yo and pull thru 2 loops on hook (2 loops on hook), (yo, insert hook in same st, yo and pull up a loop, yo and pull thru 2 loops on hook) 2 times (4 loops on hook), yo, pull thru all loops on hook.

4DCTOG: Yo, insert hook in indicated st, yo and pull up a loop, yo and pull thru 2 loops on hook (2 loops on hook), (yo, insert hook in same st, yo and pull up a loop, yo and pull thru 2 loops on hook) 3 times (5 loops on hook), yo, pull thru all loops on hook.

DAISY SQUARE (MAKE 2)

With brown yarn, make a magic ring, ch 1.

Rnd 1: 8 sc in ring, pull ring closed tight, join with sl st in first st (8 sts). Fasten off.

Rnd 2: join yellow in any st of Rnd 1; for **1st petal**, ch 3 (counts as 1 dc), 3dctog in same st as where your ch started, ch 2; for **remaining petals**, *4dctog in next st, ch 2* 7 times, join with sl st in top of ch-3 (8 petals). Fasten off.

Rnd 3: join light blue in any petal space; for **1st corner**, ch 5 (counts as 1 dc + ch 2), 3 dc in same petal space; 3 hdc in next petal space; for **next corner**, *(3 dc, ch 2, 3 dc) in next petal space; 3 hdc in next petal space* 3 times; to **finish**, 2 dc in same space as 1st corner, join with sl st in top of ch-3, sl st in corner space. Fasten off.

Rnd 4: join dark blue in any corner space; for **1st corner**, ch 5 (counts as 1 dc + ch 2), 2 dc in same corner space; *dc in next 9 sts, (2 dc, ch 2, 2 dc) in next corner space* 3 times; dc in next 9 sts; to **finish**, dc in same space as 1st corner; join with sl st in top of ch-3, sl st in corner space.

Rnd 5: for **1st corner,** ch 5 (counts as 1 dc + ch 2), 2 dc in same corner space; *dc in next 13 sts, (2 dc, ch 2, 2 dc) in next corner space* 3 times; dc in next 13 sts; to **finish**, dc in same space as 1st corner, join with sl st in top of ch-3, sl st in corner space. Fasten off.

STRAPS (MAKE 2)

With dark blue yarn, ch 7; sc in second ch from hook and in each remaining ch across (6 sts). Fasten off.

FINISHING

For **neckline**, fold one corner down 1/2" on each square and sew in place.

For **underarm seam**, stack squares with wrong sides facing and sew together for 1" as shown below.

Sew **straps** right side up to front of blouse at neckline. Sew one half of snap fasteners to back end of straps (on right side) and the other halves to back of blouse at neckline (on wrong side). Weave in ends.

Jacket

The jacket is sized generously to be worn over other clothes. The shape is created by 4 corners. Each corner is made with a (dc, ch 1, dc) stitch combination.

Sometimes the pattern will instruct you to work into a "chain-one space" (ch-1 sp) instead of into a particular stitch. Simply put, a chain space is a hole in your work that is created by making a chain. In this case, the (dc, ch 1, dc) creates the hole.

SUPPLIES

G6/4mm crochet hook

40 yds of DK, Light Worsted yarn

3 buttons, 3/8"

Sewing thread

Note: A chain 1 at the beginning of a row is for turning your work and does not count as a stitch.

Ch 32.

Row 1: ch 1, turn, dc in next 4 chs; for **corner**, (dc, ch 1, dc) in next ch; dc in next 6 chs; for **corner**, (dc, ch 1, dc) in next ch; dc in next 8 chs; for **corner**, (dc, ch 1, dc) in next ch; dc in next 6 chs; for **corner**, (dc, ch 1, dc) in next ch; dc in next 4 chs (36 sts, 4 chs).

Row 2: ch 1, turn, dc in next 5 sts; for **corner**, (dc, ch 1, dc) in next ch-1 sp; dc in next 8 sts; for **corner**, (dc, ch 1, dc) in next ch-1 sp; dc in next 10 sts; for **corner**, (dc, ch 1, dc) in next ch-1 sp; dc in next 8 sts; for **corner**, (dc, ch 1, dc) in next ch-1 sp; dc in next 5 sts (44 sts, 4 chs).

Row 3: ch 1, turn, dc in next 6 sts; for **corner**, (dc, ch 1, dc) in next ch-1 sp; dc in next 10 sts; for **corner**, (dc, ch 1, dc) in next ch-1 sp; dc in next 12 sts; for **corner**, (dc, ch 1, dc) in next ch-1 sp; dc in next 10 sts; for **corner**, (dc, ch 1, dc) in next ch-1 sp; dc in next 6 sts (52 sts, 4 chs).

Row 4: ch 1, turn, dc in next 7 sts; for **corner**, (dc, ch 1, dc) in next ch-1 sp; dc in next 12 sts; for **corner**, (dc, ch 1, dc) in next ch-1 sp; dc in next 14 sts; for **corner**, (dc, ch 1, dc) in next ch-1 sp; dc in next 12 sts; for **corner**, (dc, ch 1, dc) in next ch-1 sp; dc in next 7 sts (60 sts, 4 chs).

Row 5: ch 1, turn, dc in next 8 sts; for **corner**, (dc, ch 1, dc) in next ch-1 sp; dc in next 14 sts; for **corner**, (dc, ch 1, dc) in next ch-1 sp; dc in next 16 sts; for **corner**, (dc, ch 1, dc) in next ch-1 sp; dc in next 14 sts; for **corner**, (dc, ch 1, dc) in next ch-1 sp; dc in next 8 sts (68 sts, 4 chs).

Row 6: ch 1, turn, dc in next 9 sts; for **corner**, (dc, ch 1, dc) in next ch-1 sp; dc in next 16 sts; for **corner**, (dc, ch 1, dc) in next ch-1 sp; dc in next 18 sts; for **corner**, (dc, ch 1, dc) in next ch-1 sp; dc in next 16 sts; for **corner**, (dc, ch 1, dc) in next ch-1 sp; dc in next 9 sts (76 sts, 4 chs).

Row 7: ch 1, turn, *dc in next 4 sts, 2 dc in next st* twice; for **sleeve**, (dc, ch 2) in next ch-1 sp, skip next 18 sts, dc in next ch-1 sp; *dc in next 4 sts, 2 dc in next st* 4 times; for **sleeve**, (dc, ch 2) in next ch-1 sp, skip next 18 sts, dc in next ch-1 sp; *2 dc in next st, dc in next 4 sts* twice (52 sts, 4 chs).

Row 8: ch 1, turn, *dc in next 6 sts, 2 dc in next st* 8 times (64 sts).

Rows 9-10: ch 1, turn, dc in each st across.

FINISHING

Sew buttons to one side of front. Use spaces between sts on opposite side for buttonholes.

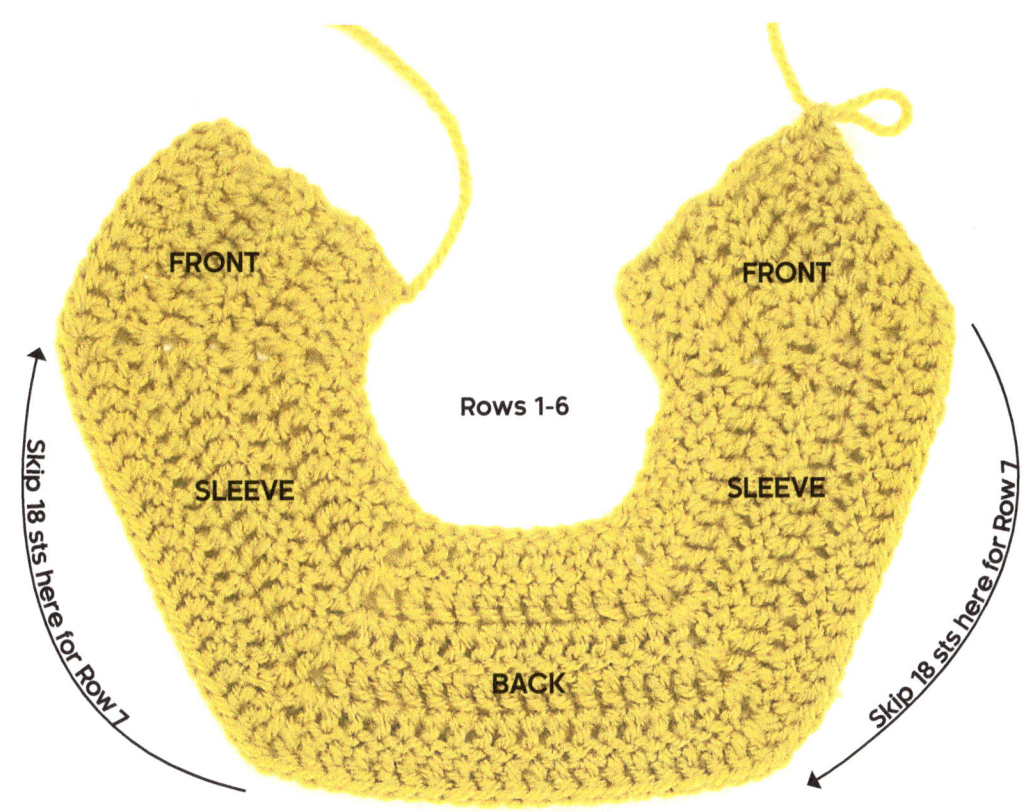

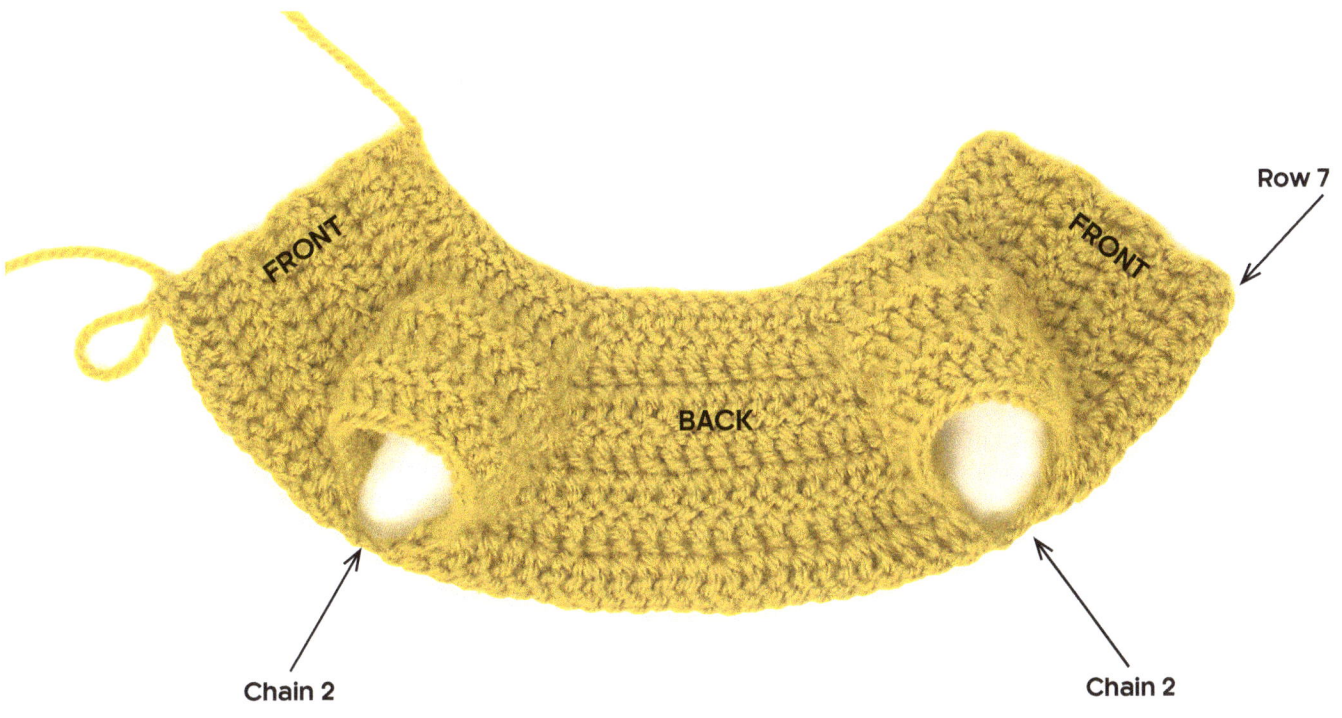

Honey Bear Blouse

This cute blouse for Honey Pie features her best friend, Honey Bear. When assembling small pieces such as this applique, I like to use sewing thread instead of the yarn tail because it is more discreet.

SUPPLIES

F5/3.75mm and G6/4mm crochet hooks

Small amount of DK, Light Worsted yarn in green, tan & cream

3 black beads, 4mm

Sewing thread

BLOUSE

With G6/4mm crochet hook and green yarn, follow instructions for Basic Blouse (see page 19).

BEAR APPLIQUE

HEAD

With F5/3.75mm crochet hook and tan yarn, make a magic ring, ch 1.

Rnd 1: 6 sc in ring, pull ring closed tight (6 sts).

Rnd 2: 2 sc in each st around. Place marker for beginning of rnd and move marker up as each rnd is completed (12 sts).

Rnd 3: *sc in next st, 2 sc in next st* 6 times (18 sts).

Rnd 4: *2 sc in next st, sc in next 2 sts* 6 times (24 sts).

Do not fasten off. Sl st in next st, for **1st Ear**, (loosely hdc, dc, hdc) in next st; sl st in next 5 sts; for **2nd Ear**, (loosely hdc, dc, hdc) in next st; sl st in next st. Fasten off.

SNOUT

With F5/3.75mm crochet hook and cream yarn, make a magic ring, ch 1.

Rnd 1: 6 sc in ring, pull ring closed tight (6 sts).

Rnd 2: 2 sc in each st around (12 sts).

Sl st in next st. Fasten off.

FINISHING

Sew snout to head as pictured. Sew beads in place for eyes and nose. Sew applique to front of blouse with sewing thread.

Drawstring Shorts

WAISTBAND

Join green yarn with sc at center front.

Row 14: sc in each st around.

Row 15: ch 1, turn, dc in each st around.

Fasten off.

FINISHING

For **drawstring**, chain a string 13" long with tan yarn. Starting at center front, weave drawstring thru dc sts of waistband. Trim tails of drawstring to 1/2".

For **decorative topstitching** around leg openings, work surface sl st from wrong side: Turn shorts inside out so that wrong side faces you. Starting at inner leg seam, insert hook in st at bottom edge, yarn over and pull up a loop of tan yarn (1 loop on hook), *insert hook in next st, yarn over and pull loop thru fabric and thru loop on hook* around. Fasten off. Weave in ends.

Note: You will yarn over on the back side of the work and bring the loop thru to the front side of the work.

The shorts are very easy to make from 2 rectangles. The rectangles are sewn together, then a waistband is worked at the top.

SUPPLIES

G6/4mm crochet hook

Small amount of DK, Light Worsted yarn in green and tan

Note: A chain 1 at the beginning of a row is for turning your work and does not count as a stitch.

SIDES (MAKE 2)

Ch 13 loosely with green yarn.

Rows 1-12: ch 1, turn, dc in each st across (13 sts).

Row 13: ch 1, do not turn, continue working forward to sc in each st across next side. This will be bottom of shorts. Fasten off.

Place pieces side-by-side. For **center front** seam, sew top 10 sts together (see dotted line in photo below). Repeat for **center back** seam. To form **legs**, sew first and last rows together on each side.

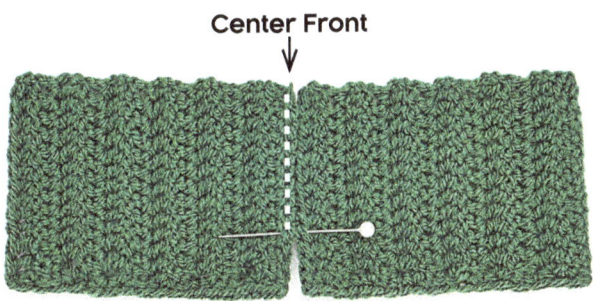

Butterfly Jeans

SUPPLIES

F5/3.75mm and G6/4mm crochet hooks

Small amount of DK, Light Worsted yarn in blue (jeans) and assorted colors (butterflies)

Stretch Magic clear elastic bead cord (.7mm)

Note: A chain 1 at the beginning of a row is for turning your work and does not count as a stitch.

SIDES (MAKE 2)

With G6/4mm crochet hook and blue yarn, ch 30 loosely.

Rows 1-12: ch 1, turn, dc in each st across (30 sts).

Row 13: ch 1, do not turn, continue working forward to sc in each st across next side. This will be bottom of jeans. Fasten off.

Place pieces side-by-side (refer to photo for Drawstring Shorts on previous page). For **center front** seam, sew top 10 sts together. Repeat for **center back** seam. To form **legs**, sew first and last rows together on each side.

WAISTBAND

With G6/4mm crochet hook and blue yarn, join with sc at center back.

Rnd 1: sc in each st around. Fasten off. Weave in ends.

BUTTERFLY APPLIQUES (MAKE 3)

With F5/3.75mm crochet hook, make a magic ring, ch 2.

Rnd 1: hdc in ring, ch 2, sl st in 2nd ch from hook, ch 1, sl st in ring, ch 3, sl st in 2nd ch from hook, ch 3, sl st in ring, ch 3, sl st in 2nd ch from hook, hdc in ring, ch 3, sl st in ring. Fasten off. Pull ring closed tight. Tie tails together.

For body/antennae, wrap contrasting yarn tightly around center twice and knot at top for butterfly's head; trim tails to 3/8". Dip tips in white glue to prevent fraying if desired. (Use a clothes pin to hold wings out of the way.)

Sew yarn tails of butterfly to center of wrong side with one tail on each side of body. These will be used to tie butterfly to jeans.

FINISHING

Tie butterflies to jeans as pictured. Thread a yarn needle with elastic cord and weave thru back of stitches around waistband. Try jeans on doll to get the right tension and knot ends of elastic together.

Fancy Pants

This is a cropped-length pant. Follow instructions for Butterfly Jeans but use a shorter starting ch of 24 ch. For **hem trim**, join contrasting color at lower edges with G6/4mm crochet hook, *5 sc in next st, skip 1 st, sl st in next st* around. Fasten off. Weave in ends.

Button-Front Skirt

The skirt is made from the top down. The pattern starts with rows to make an opening at the back. The skirt section is then made with joined rounds.

SUPPLIES

G6/4mm crochet hook

52 yds of DK, Light Worsted yarn

4 buttons, 1/2" - 5/8"

Sewing thread

Note: A chain 1 at the beginning of a row is for turning your work and does not count as a stitch.

SKIRT

Ch 30.

Rows 1-4: ch 1, turn, hdc in each st across (30 sts).

Row 5: ch 1, turn, 2 dc in each st across; sl st to first st to join (60 sts).

Now work in joined rounds.

Rnds 6-11: ch 1, do not turn, dc in each st around; sl st to first st to join.

Fasten off.

PLACKET

Ch 16.

Rows 1-4: ch 1, turn, sc in each st across (16 sts).

Row 5: ch 1, do not turn, sc in each st around next 2 sides. Fasten off.

FINISHING

Sew placket to center front as pictured. Sew 3 buttons on placket. Sew a button to one side of waistband at back opening. Use gap in sts on opposite side for buttonhole. Weave in ends.

Simple Skirt

Follow the instructions for Button-Front Skirt but omit the placket and front buttons.

Espadrilles

This pattern starts by working around a foundation chain. Tan yarn creates the look of a rope sole.

SUPPLIES

G6/4mm crochet hook

Small amount of DK Light Worsted yarn in purple and tan

With tan yarn, ch 6.

Rnd 1: for **sole**, starting in 2nd ch from hook, sc in next 4 ch, 3 sc in next ch, sc in next 3 ch, 2 sc in last ch. Place marker for beginning of rnd and move marker up as each rnd is completed (12 sts).

Rnd 2: 2 sc in next st, sc in next 3 sts, 2 sc in next 3 sts, sc in next 3 sts, 2 sc in next 2 sts (18 sts).

Rnd 3: 2 sc in next st, sc in next 4 sts, 2 sc in next st, *sc in next st, 2 sc in next st* twice, sc in next 4 sts, *2 sc in next st, sc in next st* twice (24 sts).

Rnd 4: working in **back loops only**, sc in each st around; change to purple in last st.

Rnds 5-7: resuming work in **both loops**, sc in each st around.

Rnd 8: sc in next 8 sts, sc2tog 4 times, sc in next 8 sts (20 sts).

Rnd 9: sc in next 7 sts, sc2tog 3 times, sc in next 7 sts (17 sts).

Sl st in next st. Fasten off.

For **second sole**, repeat Rnds 1-3. Do not fasten off. Place wrong side against bottom of shoe and align so that edges meet. Sl st soles together working thru both loops of second sole and unworked front loops of first sole. Fasten off. Weave in ends.

Make a second identical shoe.

Ballet Flats

This basic style can also be used to make slippers for your doll.

SUPPLIES

G6/4mm crochet hook

Small amount of DK Light Worsted yarn

Ch 6.

Rnd 1: for **sole**, starting in 2nd ch from hook, sc in next 4 ch, 3 sc in next ch, sc in next 3 ch, 2 sc in last ch. Place marker for beginning of rnd and move marker up as each rnd is completed (12 sts).

Rnd 2: 2 sc in next st, sc in next 3 sts, 2 sc in next 3 sts, sc in next 3 sts, 2 sc in next 2 sts (18 sts).

Rnd 3: 2 sc in next st, sc in next 4 sts, 2 sc in next st, *sc in next st, 2 sc in next st* twice, sc in next 4 sts, *2 sc in next st, sc in next st* twice (24 sts).

Rnd 4: working in **back loops only**, sc in each st around.

Rnds 5-7: resuming work in **both loops**, sc in each st around.

Rnd 8: sc in next 8 sts, sc2tog 4 times, sc in next 8 sts (20 sts).

Rnd 9: sl st in each st around.

Fasten off.

Make a second identical shoe.

Sandals

SUPPLIES

G6/4mm crochet hook

Small amount of DK Light Worsted yarn

2 sew-on snap fasteners

Sewing thread

Note: A chain 1 at the beginning of a row is for turning your work and does not count as a stitch.

RIGHT SANDAL

SOLE

Ch 6.

Rnd 1: starting in 2nd ch from hook, sc in next 4 ch, 3 sc in next ch, sc in next 3 ch, 2 sc in last ch. Place marker for beginning of rnd and move marker up as each rnd is completed (12 sts).

Rnd 2: 2 sc in next st, sc in next 3 sts, 2 sc in next 3 sts, sc in next 3 sts, 2 sc in next 2 sts (18 sts).

Rnd 3: 2 sc in next st, sc in next 4 sts, 2 sc in next st, *sc in next st, 2 sc in next st* twice, sc in next 4 sts, *2 sc in next st, sc in next st* twice (24 sts).

Fasten off. Weave in ends.

Repeat to make a 2nd identical sole but **do not fasten off**. Place the 2 soles wrong sides facing and loosely sl st together around perimeter working thru both layers. Fasten off. Weave in end.

HEEL CAP

Mark the 6 sts at center back of sole.

Row 1: working in **front loops only**, join with sc in first st, sc in next 5 sts (6 sts).

Rows 2-3: ch 1, turn, resuming work in **both loops**, sc in each st across.

Row 4: ch 1, turn, sc2tog, sc in next 2 sts, sc2tog (4 sts).

Row 5: ch 1, turn, sc in each st across; for **ankle strap**, ch 3 (4 sts, 3 chs).

Row 6: ch 1, turn, sc in each ch and st across; for **ankle strap**, ch 15 (7 sts, 15 chs).

Row 7: ch 1, turn, sc in each ch across (15 sts).

Fasten off. Sew end to heel cap with tail.

Sew one half of snap fastener to short end of ankle strap where strap meets heel cap (right side) and the other half to tip of long end of ankle strap (wrong side). Weave in ends.

TOE STRAP

Ch 11.

Row 1: ch 1, turn, sc in each st across (11 sts).

Fasten off.

Place toe strap at center front of sole with an interspace of 8 sts. Sew toe strap in place. Put sandal on doll, align center of toe strap with center front of ankle strap and sew in place. Weave in ends.

LEFT SANDAL

SOLE

Follow instructions for sole of right sandal.

HEEL CAP

Mark the 6 sts at center back of sole.

Row 1: working in **front loops only**, join with sc in first st, sc in next 5 sts (6 sts).

Rows 2-3: ch 1, turn, resuming work in **both loops**, sc in each st across.

Row 4: ch 1, turn, sc2tog, sc in next 2 sts, sc2tog (4 sts).

Row 5: ch 1, turn, sc in each st across; for **ankle strap**, ch 15 (4 sts, 15 chs).

Row 6: ch 1, turn, sc in each ch and st across; for **ankle strap**, ch 3 (19 sts, 3 chs).

Row 7: ch 1, turn, sc in each ch across (3 sts).

Fasten off. Sew end to heel cap with tail.

Sew one half of snap fastener to short end of ankle strap where strap meets heel cap (right side) and the other half to tip of long end of ankle strap (wrong side). Weave in ends.

TOE STRAP

Follow instructions for toe strap of right sandal.

Bow Barrette

SUPPLIES

G6/4mm crochet hook

Small amount of DK, Light Worsted yarn

1 bobby pin

Note: A chain 1 at the beginning of a row is for turning your work and does not count as a stitch.

Ch 9 loosely.

Rows 1-4: ch 1, turn, sc in each st across (9 sts).

Fasten off. Weave in ends.

For **center tie**, ch 3, fasten off.

FINISHING

Pinch middle of rectangle into a bow shape. Wrap **center tie** widthwise around middle with chs on top; knot tails together tightly. Trim tails short. Slide flat side of bobby pin under **center tie**.

Flower Barrette

SUPPLIES

G6/4mm crochet hook

Small amount of DK, Light Worsted yarn

1 button, 1/2"

Hot glue

1 bobby pin

Make a magic ring, ch 1.

Rnd 1: 5 sc in ring, pull ring closed tight (5 sts).

Rnd 2: (sl st, ch 2, 2 dc, ch 2, sl st) in each st around (5 petals).

Fasten off. Weave in ends.

Hold flower right-side up and bobby pin wavy-side up. Open bobby pin, scoop Rnd 1 onto wavy leg and pull until eye of bobby pin rests at edge of Rnd 1 (see photo below).

Attach button to center of flower with hot glue.

Watermelon Purse

SUPPLIES

G6/4mm crochet hook

Small amount of DK, Light Worsted yarn in peach, white, green and black

Note: A chain 1 at the beginning of a round does not count as a stitch.

With peach, make a magic ring, ch 1.

Rnd 1: 6 sc in ring, pull ring closed tight, join with sl st to first st (6 sts).

Rnd 2: ch 1, 2 sc in each st around, join with sl st to first st. Place marker for beginning of rnd and move marker up as each rnd is completed (12 sts).

Rnd 3: ch 1, *sc in next st, 2 sc in next st* 6 times, join with sl st to first st (18 sts).

Rnd 4: ch 1, sc in next st, 2 sc in next st, *sc in next 2 sts, 2 sc in next st* 5 times, sc in next st, join with sl st to first st (24 sts).

Rnd 5: ch 1, *sc in next 3 sts, 2 sc in next st* 6 times, join with sl st to first st; change to white in sl st (30 sts).

Rnd 6: ch 1, sc in next 2 sts, 2 sc in next st, *sc in next 4 sts, 2 sc in next st* 5 times, sc in next 2 sts, join with sl st to first st; change to green in sl st (36 sts).

Rnd 7: ch 1, *sc in next 5 sts, 2 sc in next st* 6 times, join with sl st to first st (42 sts).

Fasten off. Weave in ends.

For **seeds**, use black yarn to embroider 4 sts on Rnd 2 and 4 sts on Rnd 4 as pictured.

Repeat to make a 2nd identical watermelon piece.

FINISHING

Place the 2 watermelon circles together with wrong sides facing. For **handle**, ch 45 with green yarn; now **connect the circles** by working 28 sc thru sts of last rnd of both circles. Join to beginning of ch and continue sc across the ch. Sl st in next st. Fasten off. Weave in ends.

31

Tote Bag

The roomy tote bag will hold a lot of picnic supplies. It is worked in the round from the bottom up.

SUPPLIES

G6/4mm crochet hook

45 yds of Worsted weight yarn in turquoise

Small amount of Worsted weight yarn in yellow

2 buttons, 7/8" - 1" in pink

Sewing thread

Note: A chain 1 at the beginning of a row is for turning your work and does not count as a stitch.

Make a magic ring, ch 1.

Rnd 1: 6 sc in ring, pull ring closed tight (6 sts).

Rnd 2: 2 sc in each st around. Place marker for beginning of rnd and move marker up as each rnd is completed (12 sts).

Rnd 3: *sc in next st, 2 sc in next st* 6 times (18 sts).

Rnd 4: *sc in next 2 sts, 2 sc in next st* 6 times (24 sts).

Rnd 5: *sc in next 3 sts, 2 sc in next st* 6 times (30 sts).

Rnd 6: *sc in next 4 sts, 2 sc in next st* 6 times (36 sts).

Rnd 7: *sc in next 5 sts, 2 sc in next st* 6 times (42 sts).

Rnd 8: *sc in next 6 sts, 2 sc in next st* 6 times (48 sts).

Rnd 9: working in **back loops only,** sc in each st around.

Rnds 10-19: resuming work in **both loops,** sc in each st around.

Rnd 20: *sc in next 18 sts; for **handle**, ch 14, skip next 6 sts* twice (36 sts, 28 chs).

Rnd 21: sc in each st or ch around (64 sts).

Sl st in next st. Fasten off. Weave in ends.

STRAP

Leaving a long starting tail, ch 10 with yellow yarn.

Rows 1-3: ch 1, turn, sc in each st across (10 sts).

Fasten off.

For **button loop,** join yarn at end of strap that doesn't have tails, ch until the length fits snugly around your button, sl st in adjoinng corner. Fasten off. Weave in these ends only.

FINISHING

Sew a button to each side of bag in position shown in photos. On one side of bag, knot tails of strap tightly around thread that attached button to bag (see designated tails in photo above). Trim ends.

On other side, attach strap to bag with button loop.

Barbecue Apron

SUPPLIES

G6/4mm crochet hook

Small amount of DK, Light Worsted yarn in pink & purple

Note: A chain 1 at the beginning of a row is for turning your work and does not count as a stitch.

APRON

With pink, ch 8.

Row 1: ch 1, turn, sc in each st across (8 sts).

Rows 2-9: ch 1, turn, 2 sc in 1st st, sc in each st across until 1 st remains, 2 sc in last st (24 sts at end of Row 9).

Rows 10-20: ch 1, turn, sc in each st across.

Row 21: ch 1, turn, for **scallops**, *skip next 2 sts, 5 dc in next st, skip next 2 sts, sl st in next st* 4 times.

Fasten off. Weave in ends.

POCKET

With purple, ch 14.

Rows 1-6: ch 1, turn, sc in each st across (14 sts).

Row 7: ch 1, turn, for **1st scallop**, skip next st, 5 sc in next st, skip next st, sl st in next st; for **2nd scallop**, skip next 2 sts, 6 dc in next st skip next 2 sts, sl st in next st; for **3rd scallop**, skip next st, 5 sc in next st, skip next st, sl st in next st.

Fasten off. Sew to front of apron.

TIES

For **1st tie**, ch 50 with purple; join with sc to armhole edge and sc in each st along this edge; to finish tie, ch 50. Fasten off.

Repeat on other side for **2nd tie**.

Trim tails to 1/2" at ends of ties.

Nightgown

Row 3: ch 1, turn, sc in each st or ch across (28 sts)

Row 4: ch 1, turn, sc in each st across.

Row 5: 2 dc in each st across, join with sl st to first st (56 sts).

Now work in rnds. Place marker for beginning of rnd and move marker up as each rnd is completed.

Rnds 6-15: ch 1, dc in same st, dc in each remaining st around, join with sl st in first st.

Fasten off.

EDGE TRIM

Mark the 2 sts at center front of neckline.

For **neck trim**, join blue yarn with sl st at back left corner of neckline, *ch 3, skip 1 st, sl st in next st* 7 times, sl st in next st (first center front marker); for **1st tie**, ch a 6" string. Fasten off.

For **2nd tie**, ch a 6" string; join with sl st in next marked st at center front of neckline, sl st in next st, *ch 3, skip 1 st, sl st in next st* 7 times. Fasten off.

For **hem trim**, join blue yarn at center back, *ch 3, skip 1 st, sl st in next st* around. Fasten off.

FINISHING

Sew button to one back edge at opening slit. For **buttonhole**, join pink yarn at edge opposite button and make a chain long enough to go around button. Sl st in next st. Fasten off. Weave in ends.

The nightgown is worked from the top down, starting with rows for the yoke, then rounds for the skirt section. The length can easily be adjusted to make a short babydoll length or a full-length gown by decreasing or increasing the final rnds.

SUPPLIES

G6/4mm crochet hook

70 yds of DK, Light Worsted yarn in pink

Small amount of DK, Light Worsted yarn in blue

1 button, 1/2"

Sewing thread

Note: A chain 1 at the beginning of a row is for turning your work and does not count as a stitch.

With pink yarn, ch 32.

Row 1: ch 1, turn, sc in each ch across (32 sts).

Row 2: ch 1, turn, sc in next 4 sts; for **armhole**, ch 6, skip next 8 sts; sc in next 8 sts; for **armhole**, ch 6, skip next 8 sts; sc in next 4 sts (16 sts, 12 chs).

Slice-of-Pie Sleeping Bag

A slice of Honey Pie with whipped cream flowers makes a sweet sleeping bag There's enough room for Honey Bear too!

SUPPLIES

H8/5mm crochet hook
70 yds of Worsted weight yarn in tan
80 yds of Worsted weight yarn in cream

Note: A chain 1 at the beginning of a row is for turning your work and does not count as a stitch.

PIE FILLING

With tan yarn, ch 2.

Row 1: 2 hdc in 2nd ch from hook (2 sts).

Row 2: ch 1, turn, 2 hdc in each st across (4 sts).

Row 3: ch 1, turn, hdc in each st across.

Row 4: ch 1, turn, 2 hdc in first st, hdc in each st across to last st, 2 hdc in last st (6 sts).

Rows 5-37: repeat Rows 3-4 (38 sts at Row 37).

Fasten off. Weave in ends.

CRUST

With cream yarn, ch 2.

Row 1: 2 hdc in 2nd ch from hook (2 sts).

Row 2: ch 1, turn, 2 hdc in each st across (4 sts).

Row 3: ch 1, turn, hdc in each st across.

Row 4: ch 1, turn, 2 hdc in first st, hdc in each st across to last st, 2 hdc in last st (6 sts).

Rows 5-37: repeat Rows 3-4 (38 sts at Row 37).

Row 38: ch 1, turn, for **scalloped edge**, *sc in next st, skip next st, 6 dc in next st, skip next st* 9 times, sc2tog.

Fasten off. Weave in ends.

WHIPPED CREAM FLOWERS (MAKE 5)

With cream yarn, ch 3. Work all sts of Rnd 1, except the chs, into 3rd ch from hook.

Rnd 1: 2 dc, ch 2, sl st, *ch 2, 2 dc, ch 2, sl st* 4 times.

Fasten off. Pull tails tight.

Sew flowers to top of pie filling as pictured.

FINISHING

Starting at tips of triangles, pin pieces together with wrong side of pie filling against right side of crust and Rows 1-37 lined up. Join tan yarn with single crochet at top left corner of pie filling. Working thru both layers, work 1 row of sc around perimeter to connect pie filling with crust, making 3 sts in same st at tip. Fasten off. Weave in ends.

Picnic Blanket

Notes:

- A chain 1 at the beginning of a row is for turning your work and does not count as a stitch.

- To change color, work last stitch of old color to last yarn over, yarn over with new color and pull through both loops to complete the stitch.

- Carry unused color across top of previous row and crochet over it to encase the strand. Pink yarn will be carried along for the entire project. Red and cream will be cut after each 5-row stripe and woven in later.

- Pull gently on the strand you are carrying after each color change to remove excess slack.

Each check of the picnic blanket is 5 sts wide and 5 rows high. When doing color work such as this, the yarn tends to tangle. Check your working yarn at the end of each row and untwist as needed; or, to prevent tangles, keep one color to the front and one color to the back. For a video demo of this technique, visit my Amigurumi Tutorials board on Pinterest (see page 73).

SUPPLIES

H8/5mm crochet hook

350 yds of Worsted weight yarn in pink

290 yds of Worsted weight yarn in red

180 yds of Worsted weight yarn in cream

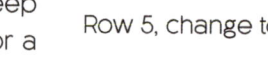

SIZE 17" x 18"

With red yarn, ch 75.

Rows 1-5: ch 1, turn, *sc with red in next 5 sts, sc with pink in next 5 sts* 7 times, sc with red in last 5 sts. In last st of Row 5, change to pink (75 sts). Cut off red with 4" tail.

Rows 6-10: ch 1, turn, *sc with pink in next 5 sts, sc with cream in next 5 sts* 7 times, sc with pink in last 5 sts. In last st of Row 10, change to red. Cut off cream with 4" tail.

Rows 11-15: ch 1, turn, *sc with red in next 5 sts, sc with pink in next 5 sts* 7 times, sc with red in last 5 sts. In last st of Row 15, change to pink. Cut off red with 4" tail.

Rows 16-20: ch 1, turn, *sc with pink in next 5 sts, sc with cream in next 5 sts* 7 times, sc with pink in last 5 sts. In last st of Row 20, change to red. Cut off cream with 4" tail.

Rows 21-25: ch 1, turn, *sc with red in next 5 sts, sc with pink in next 5 sts* 7 times, sc with red in last 5 sts. In last st of Row 25, change to pink. Cut off red with 4" tail.

Rows 26-30: ch 1, turn, *sc with pink in next 5 sts, sc with cream in next 5 sts* 7 times, sc with pink in last 5 sts. In last st of Row 30, change to red. Cut off cream with 4" tail.

Rows 31-35: ch 1, turn, *sc with red in next 5 sts, sc with pink in next 5 sts* 7 times, sc with red in last 5 sts. In last st of Row 35, change to pink. Cut off red with 4" tail.

Rows 36-40: ch 1, turn, *sc with pink in next 5 sts, sc with cream in next 5 sts* 7 times, sc with pink in last 5 sts. In last st of Row 40, change to red. Cut off cream with 4" tail.

Rows 41-45: ch 1, turn, *sc with red in next 5 sts, sc with pink in next 5 sts* 7 times, sc with red in last 5 sts. In last st of Row 45, change to pink. Cut off red with 4" tail.

Rows 46-50: ch 1, turn, *sc with pink in next 5 sts, sc with cream in next 5 sts* 7 times, sc with pink in last 5 sts. In last st of Row 50, change to red. Cut off cream with 4" tail.

Rows 51-55: ch 1, turn, *sc with red in next 5 sts, sc with pink in next 5 sts* 7 times, sc with red in last 5 sts. In last st of Row 55, change to pink. Cut off red with 4" tail.

Rows 56-60: ch 1, turn, *sc with pink in next 5 sts, sc with cream in next 5 sts* 7 times, sc with pink in last 5 sts. In last st of Row 60, change to red. Cut off cream with 4" tail.

Rows 61-65: ch 1, turn, *sc with red in next 5 sts, sc with pink in next 5 sts* 7 times, sc with red in last 5 sts. In last st of Row 65, change to pink. Cut off red with 4" tail.

Rows 66-70: ch 1, turn, *sc with pink in next 5 sts, sc with cream in next 5 sts* 7 times, sc with pink in last 5 sts. In last st of Row 70, change to red. Cut off cream with 4" tail.

Rows 71-75: ch 1, turn, *sc with red in next 5 sts, sc with pink in next 5 sts* 7 times, sc with red in last 5 sts.

Fasten off pink (do not fasten off red). Weave in ends.

FINISHING

For **border**, continue with red yarn working around the entire perimeter.

Rnd 1: ch 1, sc in each st around making 3 sts in same st at corners. Join with sl st to 1st st.

Rnd 2: ch 1, turn, sc in each st around making 3 sts in same st at corners. Fasten off. Weave in end.

Barbecue Pit Play Mat

The fire portion of the barbecue pit is made by holding 2 strands of DK, Light Worsted yarn together: one red and one orange. If you've never crocheted with multiple strands, just pretend you are working with a single strand and make each stitch as if you were holding one strand of yarn. That's really all there is to it. The grate is made with Worsted weight yarn. Color changes are done in the last st of every other row. Carry your unused yarn along the edge.

SUPPLIES

G6/4mm crochet hook

Small amount of DK, Light Worsted yarn in red and orange

Small amount of Worsted weight yarn in black

SIZE 6" x 7"

Note: A chain 1 at the beginning of a row is for turning your work and does not count as a stitch.

With 1 strand of red & 1 strand of orange yarn held together, ch 26.

Rows 1-2: ch 1, turn, sc in each st across; change to black yarn in last st (26 sts).

Rows 3-4: ch 1, turn, sc in each st across; change to red & orange yarn in last st.

Rows 5-6: ch 1, turn, sc in each st across; change to black yarn in last st.

Rows 7-8: ch 1, turn, sc in each st across; change to red & orange yarn in last st.

Rows 9-10: ch 1, turn, sc in each st across; change to black yarn in last st.

Rows 11-12: ch 1, turn, sc in each st across; change to red & orange yarn in last st.

Rows 13-14: ch 1, turn, sc in each st across; change to black yarn in last st.

Rows 15-16: ch 1, turn, sc in each st across; change to red & orange yarn in last st.

Rows 17-18: ch 1, turn, sc in each st across; change to black yarn in last st.

Rows 19-20: ch 1, turn, sc in each st across; change to red & orange yarn in last st.

Rows 21-22: ch 1, turn, sc in each st across; change to black yarn in last st.

Now work in rnds for the border.

Rnd 23: ch 1, sc in each st around making 3 sts in same st at corners.

Rnd 24: sc in each st around making 3 sts in same st at corners.

Fasten off. Weave in ends.

Picnic Basket

A little box is made from thin cardboard to give the picnic basket structure. Crocheted fabric is then glued to the box. A full-sized template for the cardboard base and a checked lining are provided at the back of the book.

Note: A chain 1 at the beginning of a row is for turning your work and does not count as a stitch.

SUPPLIES

G6/4mm crochet hook

Small amount of Worsted-weight yarn

2 buttons, 7/8" - 1"

Thin cardboard (cereal box)

Clear-drying all-purpose glue stick

Non-serrated table knife, butter knife or paper-scoring tool

Sewing thread

Clothespins

CARDBOARD BASE

1. Cut cardboard to 6 1/2" x 8".

2. Cut out or copy the **Checked Paper** on page 71.

3. Apply glue stick to cardboard and fasten to center of checked paper. Wrap excess paper to opposite side so that edges of cardboard are encased and glue in place.

Now refer to **Picnic Basket Template** on page 69.

4. Score 2" from edges (see **all** dotted lines on Template).

5. Cut along **red** dotted lines (see Template).

6. Fold cardboard up along scored lines (see arrows on Template) and crease firmly.

7. Cut off 3/4" from edges X of Overlaps (see gray areas of Template).

8. Shape cardboard into box and glue Overlaps to outside of Ends. Use clothespins to hold box in shape until glue dries.

SIDES & BOTTOM

This piece should measure 4 1/4" x 7" to fit the base. Check your work and adjust if needed.

Ch 20.

Rows 1-37: ch 1, turn, sc in each st across (20 sts).

Fasten off. Weave in ends.

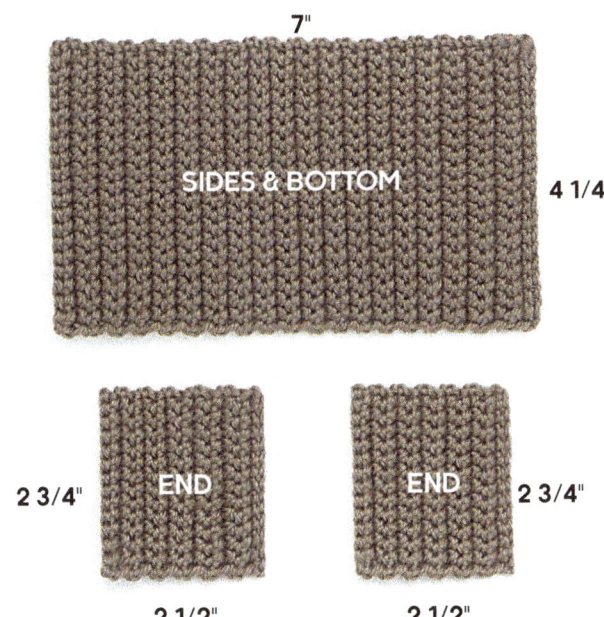

ENDS (MAKE 2)

These pieces should measure 2 3/4" x 2 1/2" to fit the base. Check your work and adjust if needed.

Ch 13.

Rows 1-12: ch 1, turn, sc in each st across (13 sts).

Fasten off. Weave in ends.

HANDLE

Leaving a long starting tail, ch 30.

Rows 1-4: ch 1, turn, sc in each st across (30 sts).

For **button loop**, ch until the length fits snugly around your button, sl st in adjoining corner, fasten off. For 2nd **button loop**, insert hook in st at base of starting tail, pull up a loop from the tail, ch until the length fits snugly around your button, sl st in adjoining corner, fasten off. Weave in ends.

FINISHING

Sew buttons to center of sides, about 5/8" from top edge. If your buttons have holes rather than a shank, make a shank with thread when you sew on the button as follows: Lay a round toothpick on top of the button and sew over the toothpick while sewing on the button to create slack. Remove toothpick, pull up on button, bring needle out below button, wind thread around slack between button and fabric about 10 times, secure end with a knot.

Glue sides/bottom piece, then end pieces, to cardboard base. Hold fabric in place with clothespins until dry. Sew corner edges together with thread.

Attach handle to basket with button loops.

Cheeseburger

For veggie burgers, make the patty in a golden-brown tone. A tweed or flecked yarn would be especially nice.

SUPPLIES

F5/3.75mm crochet hook

Small amount of DK, Light Worsted yarn in tan, brown, yellow, red and green

BUN (MAKE 2)

With tan yarn, make a magic ring, ch 1.

Rnd 1: 6 sc in ring, pull ring closed tight (6 sts).

Rnd 2: 2 sc in each st around. Place marker for beginning of rnd and move marker up as each rnd is completed (12 sts).

Rnd 3: *sc in next st, 2 sc in next st* 6 times (18 sts).

Rnd 4: *sc in next 2 sts, 2 sc in next st* 6 times (24 sts).

Rnd 5: *sc in next 3 sts, 2 sc in next st* 6 times (30 sts).

Rnd 6: sc in each st around.

Rnd 7: working in **back loops only**, *sc in next 3 sts, sc2tog* 6 times (24 sts).

Rnd 8: resuming work in **both loops**, *sc in next 2 sts, sc2tog* 6 times (18 sts).

Rnd 9: *sc in next st, sc2tog* 6 times (12 sts).

Rnd 10: sc2tog 6 times (6 sts).

Fasten off. Thread ending tail onto needle, insert needle thru front loop of each st around opening and pull tight to close hole, push needle up thru center of Rnd 1 then down between layers to hide end.

BURGER PATTY

With brown yarn, make a magic ring, ch 1.

Rnd 1: 6 sc in ring, pull ring closed tight (6 sts).

Rnd 2: 2 sc in each st around. Place marker for beginning of rnd and move marker up as each rnd is completed (12 sts).

Rnd 3: *sc in next st, 2 sc in next st* 6 times (18 sts).

Rnd 4: *sc in next 2 sts, 2 sc in next st* 6 times (24 sts).

Rnd 5: *sc in next 3 sts, 2 sc in next st* 6 times (30 sts).

Rnd 6: sc in each st around.

Rnd 7: *sc in next 3 sts, sc2tog* 6 times (24 sts).

Rnd 8: *sc in next 2 sts, sc2tog* 6 times (18 sts).

Rnd 9: *sc in next st, sc2tog* 6 times (12 sts).

Rnd 10: sc2tog 6 times (6 sts).

Fasten off. Thread ending tail onto needle, insert needle thru front loop of each stitch around opening and pull tight to close hole. Flatten into patty shape. Weave in end.

CHEESE

With yellow yarn, ch 6.

Rows 1-6: ch 1, turn, sc in each st across (6 sts). Fasten off. Use tails to sew cheese to patty if desired. Weave in ends.

41

TOMATO

The tomato is made with joined rounds.

With red yarn, make a magic ring, ch 1.

Rnd 1: 6 sc in ring, pull ring closed tight, join with sl st to first st (6 sts).

Rnd 2: ch 1, 2 sc in each st around, join with sl st to first st. Place marker for beginning of rnd and move marker up as each rnd is completed (12 sts).

Rnd 3: ch 3 (counts as dc), dc in same stitch as where your ch started, ch 1, skip next st, *2 dc in next st, ch 1, skip next st* 5 times, join with sl st to top of ch-3 (12 sts, 6 chs).

Rnd 4: ch 1, **working loosely**, *sc between next pair of dc, 2 sc in next ch-1 space* around (18 sts).

Sl st in next st. Fasten off. Weave in ends.

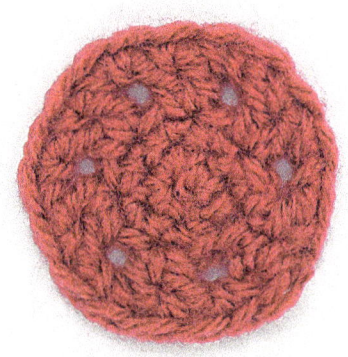

LETTUCE

With green yarn, make a magic ring, ch 1.

Rnd 1: 6 sc in ring, pull ring closed tight (6 sts).

Rnd 2: 2 sc in each st around. Place marker for beginning of rnd and move marker up as each rnd is completed (12 sts).

Rnd 3: *sc in next st, 2 sc in next st* 6 times (18 sts).

Rnd 4: *sc in next 2 sts, 2 sc in next st* 6 times (24 sts).

Rnd 5: *sc in next st, 3 sc in next st* around (48 sts).

Sl st in next st. Fasten off. Weave in ends.

Chicken Drumstick

SUPPLIES

F5/3.75mm crochet hook

Small amount of DK, Light Worsted yarn in gold and brown

Stuffing

With brown yarn, make a magic ring, ch 1.

Rnd 1: 6 sc in ring, pull ring closed tight (6 sts).

Rnd 2: 2 sc in each st around. Place marker for beginning of rnd and move marker up as each rnd is completed (12 sts).

Rnd 3: sc in each st around.

Rnd 4: *sc2tog, sc in next st* 4 times; change to gold in last st (8 sts).

Rnd 5: sc in each sc around.

Rnd 6: *sc in next st, 2 sc in next st* 4 times (12 sts).

Rnd 7: sc in each st around.

Rnd 8: *sc in next 2 sts, 2 sc in next st* 4 times (16 sts).

Rnd 9: sc in each st around.

Rnd 10: *sc in next 3 sts, 2 sc in next st* 4 times (20 sts).

Rnd 11: sc in each st around.

Rnd 12: *sc in next 2 sts, sc2tog* 5 times (15 sts).

Rnd 13: sc in each st around.

Stuff the tip.

Rnd 14: *sc in next st, sc2tog* 5 times (10 sts).

Rnd 15: sc in each st around.

Rnd 16: sc2tog 5 times (5 sts).

Fasten off. Finish stuffing drumstick. Thread ending tail onto needle, insert needle thru front loop of each stitch around opening and pull tight to close hole. Weave in end.

Corn on the Cob

A removable husk makes the corn extra fun for play. A hole at the bottom of the husk accommodates the stalk.

SUPPLIES

F5/3.75mm crochet hook

Small amount of DK, Light Worsted yarn in yellow and green

Stuffing

EAR

With yellow yarn, make a magic ring, ch 1.

Rnd 1: 6 sc in ring, pull ring closed tight (6 sts).

Rnd 2: working in **back loops only,** 2 sc in each st around. Place marker for beginning of rnd and move marker up as each rnd is completed (12 sts).

Rnds 3-4: resuming work in **both loops,** sc in each st around.

Rnd 5: sc in next 10 sts, sc2tog (11 sts).

Rnd 6: sc in each st around.

Rnd 7: sc in next 9 sts, sc2tog (10 sts).

Rnd 8: sc in each st around.

Rnd 9: sc in next 8 sts, sc2tog (9 sts).

Rnd 10: sc in each st around.

Rnd 11: sc in next 7 sts, sc2tog (8 sts).

Rnd 12: sc in each st around.

Rnd 13: sc in next 6 sts, sc2tog (7 sts).

Rnd 14: sc in next 5 sts, sc2tog (6 sts).

Rnd 15: sc in next 4 sts, sc2tog (5 sts).

Fasten off. Stuff the corn. Thread ending tail onto needle, insert needle thru front loop of each stitch around opening and pull tight to close hole.

STALK

Rnd 1: join green yarn with sc in an unworked front loop of Rnd 2 of Ear, sc in each remaining front loop around (6 sts).

Rnds 2-3: resuming work in **both loops,** sc in each st around.

Fasten off. Stuff stalk. Thread ending tail onto needle, insert needle thru front loop of each stitch around opening and pull tight to close hole. Weave in ends.

HUSK

Ch 9 with green yarn, join with sl st to 1st ch to make a ring using care not to twist the chain.

Rnd 1: 2 sc in each ch around. Place marker for beginning of rnd and move marker up as each rnd is completed (18 sts).

Rnds 2-4: sc in each st around.

Rnd 5: *sc in next st, sc2tog* 6 times (12 sts).

Do not fasten off.

For **leaves**, change to working in rows. Three leaves will be worked into Rnd 5.

Note: A chain 1 at the beginning of a row is for turning your work and does not count as a stitch.

FIRST LEAF

Row 1: sc in next 4 sts (4 sts).

Rows 2-4: ch 1, turn, sc in each st across.

Row 5: ch 1, turn, sc in next 2 sts, sc2tog (3 sts).

Rows 6-7: ch 1, turn, sc in each st across.

Row 8: ch 1, turn, sc in next st, sc2tog (2 sts).

Row 9: ch 1, turn, sc in each st across.

Row 10: ch 1, turn, sc2tog (1 st).
Fasten off.

SECOND LEAF

Row 1: join green yarn with sc in next st of Rnd 5, sc in next 3 sts (4 sts).

Rows 2-10: make the same as First Leaf.
Fasten off.

THIRD LEAF

Row 1: join green yarn with sc in next st of Rnd 5, sc in next 3 sts (4 sts).

Rows 2-10: make the same as First Leaf.

Do not fasten off. Sc in each st around leaves making 3 sts in same st at tips.

Fasten off. Weave in ends.

Watermelon Slice

The watermelon slice is stuffed only with the yarn tails.

SUPPLIES

F5/3.75mm crochet hook

Small amount of DK, Light Worsted yarn in peach, white, green and black

With peach yarn, make a magic ring, ch 1.

Rnd 1: 6 sc in ring, pull ring closed tight (6 sts).

Rnd 2: 2 sc in each st around. Place marker for beginning of rnd and move marker up as each rnd is completed (12 sts).

Rnd 3: *sc in next st, 2 sc in next st* 6 times (18 sts).

Rnd 4: *sc in next 2 sts, 2 sc in next st* 6 times (24 sts).

Rnd 5: *sc in next 3 sts, 2 sc in next st* 6 times; change to white yarn in last st (30 sts).

Rnd 6: *sc in next 4 sts, 2 sc in next st* 6 times; change to green yarn in last st (36 sts).

Rnd 7: *sc in next 5 sts, 2 sc in next st* 6 times (42 sts).

Pause to embroider seeds by making straight sts around Rnd 4 with black. Fold circle in half so that wrong sides face and stuff yarn tails inside.

Rnd 8: ch 1, sl st in each st along edge working thru both layers to close up the watermelon slice. Weave in end.

Fruit Drink

Make this picnic beverage in assorted flavors. Instructions are provided for grape. Change colors as pictured for lime and orange.

SUPPLIES

F5/3.75mm crochet hook

Small amount of DK, Light Worsted yarn in lavender, purple, white and blue (for grape drink)

Small piece of thin cardboard (cereal box weight)

Glue

With lavender yarn, make a magic ring, ch 1.

Rnd 1: 6 sc in ring, pull ring closed tight (6 sts).

Rnd 2: 2 sc in each st around. Place marker for beginning of rnd and move marker up as each rnd is completed (12 sts).

Rnd 3: *sc in next st, 2 sc in next st* 6 times (18 sts).

Rnd 4: working in **back loops only**, sc in each st around.

Rnds 5-9: resuming work in **both loops**, sc in each st around; change to white yarn in last st.

For **base**, cut a circle of cardboard the same size as bottom of bottle (see Bottle Base Template). Spread glue on cardboard disk and glue it to inside of bottle bottom. This will keep bottom flat and enable bottle to stand on its own. Stuff bottle and continue stuffing as you work.

Rnd 10: sc in each st around; change to purple yarn in last st.

Rnds 11-14: sc in each st around; change to white yarn in last st.

Rnd 15: sc in each st around; change to lavender yarn in last st.

Rnds 16-19: sc in each st around.

Rnd 20: *sc in next st, sc2tog* 6 times; change to blue yarn in last st (12 sts).

Rnd 21: *sc in next st, sc2tog* 4 times (8 sts).

Rnds 22-23: sc in each st around; change to purple yarn in last st.

Rnds 24-25: sc in each st around.

Fasten off.

FINISHING

Finish stuffing bottle. Thread ending tail onto needle, insert needle thru front loop of each stitch around opening and pull tight to close hole. Shape bottle cap as follows: Stab needle down thru center of Rnd 25 and out thru center of purple stripe. Sew back into bottle inserting needle close to point of exit and out thru bottle top. Pull gently on yarn tail to compress top and create a flat bottle cap. Sew up and down again in this manner as needed to get a nice flat cap. Weave in end.

Bottle Base Template

S'Mores

This popular picnic treat is made from a toasted marshmallow and a piece of chocolate sandwiched between 2 graham crackers. People who eat one always want "some more" and that's how they got their name. Provide a skewer for children (older kids only) to toast the marshmallow over the Barbecue Pit Play Mat. Note that Worsted weight yarn is used for the Graham Cracker and DK, Light worsted for the other components.

SUPPLIES

F5/3.75mm crochet hook

Small amount of DK, Light Worsted yarn in dark brown & white

Small amount of Worsted weight yarn in gold

Clear-drying white craft glue

Small amount of foil or wax paper

Small paint brush

Small bowl

10 brown beads, 3mm

Sewing thread

GRAHAM CRACKERS (MAKE 2)

The graham cracker is crocheted in continuous rounds, then stiffened with white glue. Your favorite brand of glue will do fine. Stiffening is very easy and the end result is perfect for this project.

With Worsted weight yarn in gold, make a magic ring, ch 1.

Rnd 1: 4 sc in ring, pull ring closed tight (4 sts).

Rnd 2: 3 sc in each st around. Place marker for beginning of rnd and move marker up as each rnd is completed (12 sts).

Rnd 3: sc in next st, 3 sc in next st, *sc in next 2 sts, 3 sc in next st* 3 times, sc in next st (20 sts).

Rnd 4: sc in next 2 sts, 3 sc in next st, *sc in next 4 sts, 3 sc in next st* 3 times, sc in next 2 sts (28 sts).

Rnd 5: sc in next 3 sts, 3 sc in next st, *sc in next 6 sts, 3 sc in next st* 3 times, sc in next 3 sts (36 sts).

Sl st in next st. Weave in ends.

With sewing needle and thread, sew beads in place on graham crackers as pictured.

Stiffen Graham Crackers as follows:

1. In a small dish, stir together a mixture of approximately 60% glue and 40% water. The mixture is very forgiving, so don't worry about measuring.

2. Place graham cracker wrong-side up on foil or wax paper. (Glue is only applied to the wrong side so that the right side retains the pretty finish of the yarn.)

3. Paint glue mixture on surface until it is well covered.

4. Let dry. Be patient—it can take several days for the glue to completely dry.

Repeat if more stiffness is desired.

Rnd 9: working in **back loops only**, *sc in next st, sc2tog* 6 times (12 sts).

Rnd 10: resuming work in **both loops**, sc2tog 6 times (6 sts).

Fasten off with extra long tail.

Stuff marshmallow. Thread ending tail onto needle, insert needle thru front loop of each stitch around opening and pull tight to close hole. Shape marshmallow as follows: Stab needle down thru center of Rnd 10 and out opposite side thru center of Rnd 1. Sew back into marshmallow a bit off-center and out at opposite side. Pull gently on yarn tail to compress marshmallow and create a flat top and bottom. Sew up and down again in this manner if needed to get a nice shape. Weave in end.

Optional: To make the marshmallow look toasted, dip a cotton swab in golden-brown eye shadow and rub lightly on surface. If color wears away from play, reapply!

CHOCOLATE SQUARE

With DK, Light Worsted yarn in brown, make a magic ring, ch 1.

Rnd 1: 4 sc in ring, pull ring closed tight (4 sts).

Rnd 2: 3 sc in each st around. Place marker for beginning of rnd and move marker up as each rnd is completed (12 sts).

Rnd 3: sc in next st, 3 sc in next st, *sc in next 2 sts, 3 sc in next st* 3 times, sc in next st (20 sts).

Rnd 4: sc in next 2 sts, 3 sc in next st, *sc in next 4 sts, 3 sc in next st* 3 times, sc in next 2 sts (28 sts).

Rnd 5: sc in next 3 sts, 3 sc in next st, *sc in next 6 sts, 3 sc in next st* 3 times, sc in next 3 sts (36 sts).

Sl st in next st. Weave in ends.

MARSHMALLOW

With DK, Light Worsted yarn in white, make a magic ring, ch 1.

Rnd 1: 6 sc in ring, pull ring closed tight (6 sts).

Rnd 2: 2 sc in each st around. Place marker for beginning of rnd and move marker up as each rnd is completed (12 sts).

Rnd 3: *sc in next st, 2 sc in next st* 6 times (18 sts).

Rnd 4: working in **back loops only**, sc in each st around.

Rnds 5-8: resuming work in **both loops**, sc in each st around.

Blueberry Pie

SUPPLIES

F5/3.75mm crochet hook

Small amount of DK, Light Worsted yarn in blue and beige

Small amount of Worsted weight yarn in gray and white

Stuffing

Note: A chain 1 at the beginning of a row is for turning your work and does not count as a stitch.

PIE SLICE (MAKE 6)

BERRY TOP

With DK, Light Worsted yarn in blue, ch 2.

Row 1: 2 sc in 2nd ch from hook (2 sts).

Row 2: ch 1, turn, 2 sc in each st across (4 sts).

Row 3: ch 1, turn, sc in each st across.

Row 4: ch 1, turn, 2 sc in next st, sc in next 2 sts, 2 sc in next st (6 sts).

Row 5: ch 1, turn, sc in each st across.

Row 6: ch 1, turn, 2 sc in next st, sc in next 4 sts, 2 sc in next st (8 sts).

Row 7: ch 1, turn, sc in each st across.

Row 8: ch 1, turn, 2 sc in next st, sc in next 6 sts, 2 sc in next st (10 sts).

Row 9: ch 1, turn, sc in each st across. Do not fasten off.

BERRY SIDES

Row 10: ch 1, do not turn, work forward to sc in each st along sides A and B (19 sts). See diagram.

Rows 11-13: ch 1, turn, sc in each st across. Fasten off.

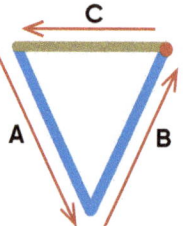

CRUST

With DK, Light Worsted yarn in beige, ch 2.

Row 1: 2 sc in 2nd ch from hook (2 sts).

Row 2: ch 1, turn, 2 sc in each st across (4 sts).

Row 3: ch 1, turn, sc in each st across.

Row 4: ch 1, turn, 2 sc in next st, sc in next 2 sts, 2 sc in next st (6 sts).

Row 5: ch 1, turn, sc in each st across.

Row 6: ch 1, turn, 2 sc in next st, sc in next 4 sts, 2 sc in next st (8 sts).

Row 7: ch 1, turn, sc in each st across.

Row 8: ch 1, turn, 2 sc in next st, sc in next 6 sts, 2 sc in next st (10 sts).

Row 9: ch 1, turn, sc in each st across.

Row 10: ch 1, turn, working in **front loops only**, sc in each st across.

Rows 11-13: ch 1, turn, resuming work in **both loops**, sc in each st across.

Next a **scalloped edge** is made—connecting the Berry and Crust layers together at the same time.

Rnd 14: ch 1, turn, place Berry Top on Crust wrong sides together. Line up the 10 sts of Berry Top, Row 9, with the 10 sts of Crust, Row 13. **For scallops,** sl st with beige yarn thru both layers in 1st st (see red dot on diagram), *5 sc in next st, skip 1 st, sl st in next st* 3 times.

Continue crocheting forward thru both layers making a sc in each st around until a small gap remains. Pause to stuff pie, then make last few sts to close gap. Fasten off. Weave in ends. Pinch pie slice into shape.

PIE PAN

With Worsted weight yarn in gray, make a magic ring, ch 1.

Rnd 1: 6 sc in ring, pull ring closed tight (6 sts).

Rnd 2: 2 sc in each st around. Place marker for beginning of rnd and move marker up as each rnd is completed (12 sts).

Rnd 3: *sc in next st, 2 sc in next st* 6 times (18 sts).

Rnd 4: *sc in next 2 sts, 2 sc in next st* 6 times (24 sts).

Rnd 5: *sc in next 3 sts, 2 sc in next st* 6 times (30 sts).

Rnd 6: *sc in next 4 sts, 2 sc in next st* 6 times (36 sts).

Rnd 7: *sc in next 5 sts, 2 sc in next st* 6 times (42 sts).

Rnd 8: *sc in next 6 sts, 2 sc in next st* 6 times (48 sts).

Rnd 9: *sc in next 7 sts, 2 sc in next st* 6 times (54 sts).

Rnd 10: *sc in next 8 sts, 2 sc in next st* 6 times (60 sts).

Rnd 11: *sc in next 9 sts, 2 sc in next st* 6 times (66 sts).

Rnd 12: working in **front loops only**, *sc in next 21 sts, 2 sc in next st* 3 times (69 sts).

Rnd 13: resuming work in **both loops**, sc in next 22 sts, 2 sc in next st* 3 times (72 sts).

Rnd 14: *sc in next 23 sts, 2 sc in next st* 3 times (75 sts).

Rnd 15: *sc in next 24 sts, 2 sc in next st* 3 times (78 sts).

Rnd 16: *sc in next 25 sts, 2 sc in next st* 3 times (81 sts).

Rnd 17: *sc in next 26 sts, 2 sc in next st* 3 times (84 sts).

Rnd 18: working in **back loops only**, sc in each st around.

Sl st in next st. Fasten off. Weave in end.

WHIPPED CREAM DOLLOP

With Worsted weight yarn in white, ch 60.

Rows 1-2: ch 1, turn, sc in each st across.

Fasten off.

Tie strip in a loose overhand knot. Repeat. Tuck in ends to finish forming a dollop shape. Weave in ends.

FINISHING

Place pie slices in pie pan with whipped cream dollop at the center.

Ketchup & Mustard

The bottle is worked in the round from the bottom up.

SUPPLIES

F5/3.75mm crochet hook

Small amount of DK, Light Worsted yarn in red and yellow

Sewing thread in red and yellow

Stuffing

BOTTLE

Make a magic ring, ch 1.

Rnd 1: 5 sc in ring, pull ring closed tight (5 sts).

Rnd 2: 2 sc in each st around. Place marker for beginning of rnd and move marker up as each rnd is complete (10 sts).

Rnd 3: *sc in next st, 2 sc in next st* 5 times (15 sts).

Rnd 4: working in **back loops only**, sc in each st around.

Rnds 5-16: resuming work in **both loops**, sc in each st around.

Start stuffing bottle.

Rnd 17: working in **back loops only**, *sc in next st, sc2tog* 5 times (10 sts).

Rnd 18: resuming work in **both loops**, sc2tog 5 times (5 sts).

Fasten off with extra long tail. Finish stuffing bottle. Thread ending tail onto needle, insert needle thru front loop of each stitch around opening and pull tight to close hole. Shape bottle as follows: Stab needle down thru center of Rnd 18 and out opposite end thru center of Rnd 1. Sew back into bottle a bit off-center and out at opposite end. Pull gently on yarn tail to compress cylinder and create a flat top and bottom. Sew up and down again in this manner as needed to get a nice shape. Weave in end.

CAP

Make a magic ring, ch 1.

Rnd 1: 5 sc in ring, pull ring closed tight (5 sts).

Rnd 2: 2 sc in each st around. Place marker for beginning of rnd and move marker up as each rnd is completed (10 sts).

Rnd 3: sc in each st around.

Rnd 4: sc2tog 5 times (5 sts).

Fasten off. Thread ending tail onto needle, insert needle thru front loop of each stitch around opening and pull tight to close hole. Flatten cap so that Rnd 1 meets Rnd 4.

SPOUT

Ch 3.

Row 1: sl st in 2nd ch from hook and in next ch (2 sts).

Fasten off.

FINISHING

Sew tails of spout down thru top of cap and tie all tails together to secure spout in place.

Sew tails of cap and spout down thru top of bottle (Rnd 18) to place cap in position and to conceal the ends. Sew cap to bottle top with thread.

Embroider K for Ketchup and M for Mustard as shown in photo.

To mark letters, copy the Templates. Cut out and place in position on bottles. Poke a pin thru paper at each end point of letters, then tear away paper. Use the pins as your guides for embroidering the stitches.

Embroidery Templates

Bag of Potato Chips

Little crinkle-cut chips are made by working in rows. A bag is worked in the round from the top down. Ultra thin double-sided Velcro is used for the closure on the bag. This makes a fun noise when the bag is opened!

SUPPLIES

F5/3.75mm crochet hook

Small amount of DK, Light Worsted yarn in yellow, bright yellow and white

4-inch piece of ultra thin double sided hook-and-loop fastener tape (Velcro) in yellow, 3/8"

Sewing thread in yellow

Note: A chain 1 at the beginning of a row is for turning your work and does not count as a stitch.

POTATO CHIPS (MAKE 8)

Ch 5 with yellow yarn.

Work in **back loops only** for the entire chip.

Row 1: ch 1, turn, sc in next 4 ch, 2 sc in last ch (6 sts).

Row 2: ch 1, turn, sc in next 5 sts, 2 sc in last st (7 sts).

Row 3: ch 1, turn, sc in next 6 sts, 2 sc in last st (8 sts).

Row 4: ch 1, turn, sc in each st across.

Row 5: ch 1, turn, sc in next 6 sts, sc2tog (7 sts).

Row 6: ch 1, turn, sc in next 5 sts, sc2tog (6 sts).

Row 7: ch 1, turn, sc in next 4 sts, sc2tog (5 sts).

Fasten off. Weave in ends around perimeter to create a rounded edge.

BAG

Ch 32 with yellow yarn, join with sl st to first ch to make a ring using care not to twist the chain.

Rnd 1: sc in each ch around. Place marker for beginning of rnd and move marker up as each rnd is completed (32 sts).

Rnds 2-3: ch 1, turn, sc in each st around, join with sl st to first st.

Rnds 4-9: sc in each st around; change to white yarn in last st.

Rnd 10: sc in each st around; change to bright yellow yarn in last st.

Rnds 11-13: sc in each st around; change to white yarn in last st.

Rnd 14: sc in each st around; change to yellow yarn in last st.

Rnds 15-22: sc in each st around.

Fasten off. Flatten bag so that jogs in stripes from color changes are at a side crease. This will make them less noticeable.

Row 23: to **close bottom**, join yellow with sc at corner of bag, sc through all layers across (16 sts).

Row 24: ch 1, turn, sc in each st across.

Fasten off. Weave in ends.

Cut two 2-inch pieces of Velcro. Place one hook-side up, the other loop-side up, and sew to inside of bag along top edges.

Hot Dog

You'll love how easy it is to make the hot dog bun!

SUPPLIES

F5/3.75mm crochet hook

Small amount of DK, Light Worsted yarn in raspberry, tan, red and yellow

Stuffing

Note: A chain 1 at the beginning of a row is for turning your work and does not count as a stitch.

HOT DOG

With raspberry yarn, make a magic ring, ch 1.

Rnd 1: 5 sc in ring, pull ring closed tight (5 sts).

Rnd 2: 2 sc in each st around. Place marker for beginning of rnd and move marker up as each rnd is completed (10 sts).

Rnds 3-11: sc in each st around.

Stuff the hot dog.

Rnd 12: sc2tog 5 times (5 sts).

Fasten off. Thread ending tail onto needle, insert needle thru front loop of each stitch around opening and pull tight to close hole. Weave in ends.

BUN

With tan yarn, ch 10.

Rows 1-10: ch 1, turn, sc in each st across (10 sts).

Now work in rounds and keep your stitches tight. You are creating a rim that will hug the hot dog.

Rnds 11-12: sc in each st around perimeter, **except** sl st instead of sc at center-sides of bun (see blue dots in photo below).

Fasten off. Weave in ends.

CONDIMENTS

With yellow yarn, make a 2" chain. Fasten off. Weave in ends. Repeat with red yarn.

Note: The condiments can be stiffened to make them easier to handle for play. Just follow the instructions for stiffening on page 46. You can stiffen the mustard and ketchup in a straight line or a wavy shape.

Vegetable Kebabs

A medley of veggies makes this a colorful dish. Older children can thread the vegetables onto a skewer for cooking on the BBQ Play Mat.

SUPPLIES

F5/3.75mm crochet hook

Small amount of DK, Light Worsted yarn in red, yellow, purple, white, light green, medium green and dark green

Thin bamboo skewers cut to 4" long (older kids only)

ZUCCHINI SLICE

With light green yarn, make a magic ring, ch 1.

Rnd 1: 6 sc in ring, pull ring closed tight (6 sts).

Rnd 2: 2 sc in each st around. Place marker for beginning of rnd and move marker up as each rnd is completed (12 sts).

Rnd 3: *sc in next st, 2 sc in next st* 6 times; change to dark green yarn in last st (18 sts).

Rnd 4: sc in each st around; change to light green yarn in last st.

Rnd 5: *sc in next st, sc2tog in next st* 6 times (12 sts).

Rnd 6: sc2tog 6 times (6 sts).

Fasten off. Flatten piece so that center of Rnd 1 meets center of Rnd 6. Trim starting tail and dark green tails to 1" and tuck inside disk. Thread ending tail onto needle, insert needle thru front loop of each stitch around opening and pull tight to close hole. Weave in end.

CHERRY TOMATO

Make some with red yarn and some with yellow yarn.

Make a magic ring, ch 1.

Rnd 1: 6 sc in ring, pull ring closed tight (6 sts).

Rnd 2: 2 sc in each st around. Place marker for beginning of rnd and move marker up as each rnd is completed (12 sts).

Rnds 3-4: sc in each st around.

Rnd 5: sc2tog 6 times; stuff piece when you are halfway around (6 sts).

Fasten off. Pack in more stuffing with eraser end of pencil. Thread ending tail onto needle, insert needle thru front loop of each stitch around opening and pull tight to close hole. Weave in end.

BELL PEPPER

Make a variety of colors with yellow, medium green and red yarn.

Make a magic ring, ch 1.

Rnd 1: 4 sc in ring, pull ring closed tight (4 sts).

Rnd 2: *sc in next st, 2 sc in next st* twice (6 sts).

Rnd 3: *sc in next 2 sts, 2 sc in next st* twice (8 sts).

Rnd 4: *sc in next 3 sts, 2 sc in next st* twice (10 sts).

Rnd 5: *sc in next 4 sts, 2 sc in next st* twice (12 sts).

Rnd 6: *sc in next 5 sts, 2 sc in next st* twice (14 sts).

Rnd 7: *sc in next 6 sts, 2 sc in next st* twice (16 sts).

Fasten off. Flatten to make a triangle shape. Trim starting tail to 1" and tuck inside. Sew end closed. Weave in end.

RED ONION

With purple yarn, make a magic ring, ch 1.

Rnd 1: 4 sc in ring, pull ring closed tight (4 sts).

Rnd 2: 3 sc in each st around. Place marker for beginning of rnd and move marker up as each rnd is completed (12 sts).

Rnd 3: sc in next st, 3 sc in next st, *sc in next 2 sts, 3 sc in next st* 3 times, sc in last st (20 sts).

Rnd 4: sc in each st around; change to white yarn in last st.

Rnd 5: sc in next st, sc3tog, *sc in next 2 sts, sc3tog* 3 times, sc in last st (12 sts).

Rnd 6: sc3tog 4 times (4 sts).

Fasten off. Flatten piece so that center of Rnd 1 meets center of Rnd 6. Trim starting tail and purple tails to 1" and tuck inside. Thread ending tail onto needle, insert needle thru front loop of each stitch around opening and pull tight to close hole. Weave in end.

Spatula

Flip and serve amigurumi burgers with this cute utensil. The spatula is crocheted in rounds from blade to handle. A simple wire frame provides a rigid structure.

SUPPLIES

G6/4mm crochet hook
Small amount of Worsted weight yarn in brown and gray
2 gold flat buttons or beads, 1/4" (6-7mm)
Sewing thread
1 piece of 18-gauge florist stem wire, 18" long
Wire cutters
Pen

BLADE & HANDLE

With gray yarn, ch 14, join with sl st to 1st ch to make a ring using care not to twist the chain.

Rnds 1-12: sc in each st around. Place marker for beginning of rnd and move marker up as each rnd is completed (14 sts).

Rnd 13: *sc in next 5 sts, sc2tog* twice (12 sts).

Rnd 14: *sc in next 4 sts, sc2tog* twice (10 sts).

Rnd 15: *sc in next 3 sts, sc2tog* twice; change to brown yarn in last st (8 sts).

Rnds 16-30: sc in each st around.

Fasten off. Flatten and sew the handle end closed. Weave in yarn tail.

FINISHING

For **wire frame**, hold barrel of pen against middle of wire and bend wire around pen to make a U-shape. Lay wire on spatula and bend into the shape of the spatula. Cut off excess wire and twist ends together to connect the frame. Pinch twisted area with pliers to flatten, if desired. Tape loose ends to frame (see photo). Slide frame into spatula. Sew blade closed. Bend spatula at red dots to get the shape of a spatula as shown in photos. For **mock rivets**, sew buttons to handle.

Bend into a U   Tape Loose Ends   Bend at Dots

Picnic Plates

Use your yarn stash to make a variety of festive colors. For rigid plates, choose a brand of yarn that is rather stiff. If more stiffness is desired, the plates can be stiffened with diluted white glue (see page 46).

SUPPLIES

G6/4mm crochet hook

Small amount of Worsted weight yarn

Note: A chain 1 at the beginning of a round does not count as a stitch.

Make a magic ring, ch 1.

Rnd 1: 6 sc in ring, pull ring closed tight, join with sl st to first st (6 sts).

Rnd 2: ch 1, 2 sc in each st around, join with sl st to first st. Place marker for beginning of rnd and move marker up as each rnd is completed (12 sts).

Rnd 3: ch 1, *sc in next st, 2 sc in next st* 6 times, join with sl st to first st (18 sts).

Rnd 4: ch 1, sc in next st, 2 sc in next st, *sc in next 2 sts, 2 sc in next st* 5 times, sc in next st, join with sl st to first st (24 sts).

Rnd 5: ch 1, *sc in next 3 sts, 2 sc in next st* 6 times, join with sl st to first st (30 sts).

Rnd 6: ch 1, sc in next 2 sts, 2 sc in next st, *sc in next 4 sts, 2 sc in next st* 5 times, sc in next 2 sts, join with sl st to first st (36 sts).

Rnd 7: ch 1, working in **front loops only**, *sc in next 5 sts, 2 sc in next st* 6 times, join with sl st to first st (42 sts).

Rnd 8: ch 1, working in **back loops only**, sc in next 3 sts, 2 sc in next st, *sc in next 6 sts, 2 sc in next st* 5 times, sc in next 3 sts, join with sl st to first st (48 sts).

Rnd 9: ch 1, resuming work in **both loops,** *sc in next 7 sts, 2 sc in next st* 6 times, join with sl st to first st (54 sts).

Fasten off. Weave in ends.

Mini FrizzBee

Rnd 3: sl st loosely in first st, 2 sc in next st, sc in next 2 sts, *sc in next st, 2 sc in next st, sc in next 2 sts* 5 times; change to yellow yarn in last st (30 sts).

Rnd 4: sl st loosely in first st, sc in next 2 sts, 2 sc in next st, sc in next st, *sc in next 3 sts, 2 sc in next st, sc in next st* 5 times; change to black yarn in last st (36 sts).

Rnd 5: sl st loosely in first st, sc in each remaining st around.

Rnd 6: sl st in each st around.

Fasten off. Weave in ends.

The Mini FrizzBee isn't just for show—it really works! Picnics are more fun with games and this little doll-sized disc (3″ diameter) soars like the big guys. It's soft enough to fly indoors, too. For the best lift, throw it angled upward.

In this pattern, you will be working with 2 strands of yarn held together. The multiple strands make a nice, sturdy structure. If you've never crocheted with multiple strands, just pretend you are working with a single strand and make each stitch as if you were holding one strand of yarn.

SUPPLIES

H8/5mm crochet hook

Small amount of Worsted weight yarn in black and yellow

Note: Hold 2 strands of yarn together for the entire pattern.

With black yarn, ch 10, join with sl st to first ch to make a ring using care not to twist the chain.

Rnd 1: 18 sc in ring; change to yellow yarn in last st (18 sts).

Rnd 2: sl st loosely in first st, sc in next st, 2 sc in next st, *sc in next 2 sts, 2 sc in next st* 5 times; change to black yarn in last st. Place marker for beginning of rnd and move marker up as each rnd is completed (24 sts).

Honey Bear

Honey Bear is Honey Pie's special friend. Pipe cleaners are optional in the bear's arms. If used, the arms are able to hold a pose. Without them, the bear is extra cuddly.

SIZE

4" tall, not including ears

SUPPLIES

G6/4mm crochet hook

Small amount of Worsted weight yarn in tan & white (bear)

Small amount of DK, Light Worsted yarn (vest)

2 black safety eyes, 6mm

1 black bead, 4mm

2 pipe cleaners in beige (optional)

Sewing thread

Stuffing

HEAD

With Worsted weight yarn in tan, make a magic ring, ch 1.

Rnd 1: 6 sc in ring, pull ring closed tight (6 sts).

Rnd 2: 2 sc in each st around. Place marker for beginning of rnd and move marker up as each rnd is completed (12 sts).

Rnd 3: *sc in next st, 2 sc in next st* 6 times (18 sts).

Rnd 4: *sc in next 2 sts, 2 sc in next st* 6 times (24 sts).

Rnd 5: *sc in next 3 sts, 2 sc in next st* 6 times (30 sts).

Rnds 6-9: sc in each st around.

Rnd 10: *sc in next 3 sts, sc2tog* 6 times (24 sts).

Rnd 11: *sc in next 2 sts, sc2tog* 6 times (18 sts).

Rnd 12: *sc in next 4 sts, sc2tog* 3 times (15 sts).

Sl st in next st. Fasten off.

Attach eyes between Rnds 7-8 with an interspace of 6 sts; or eyes may be glued in later if desired. Stuff head.

BODY

With Worsted weight yarn in tan, make a magic ring, ch 1.

Rnd 1: 6 sc in ring, pull ring closed tight (6 sts).

Rnd 2: 2 sc in each st around. Place marker for beginning of rnd and move marker up as each rnd is completed (12 sts).

Rnd 3: *sc in next st, 2 sc in next st* 6 times (18 sts).

Rnd 4: *sc in next 2 sts, 2 sc in next st* 6 times (24 sts).

Rnds 5-7: sc in each st around.

Rnd 8: *sc in next 2 sts, sc2tog* 6 times (18 sts).

Rnds 9-10: sc in each st around.

Rnd 11: *sc in next 4 sts, sc2tog* 3 times (15 sts).

Rnd 12: sc in each st around.

Sl st in next st. Fasten off.

Stuff body. Sew body to head.

EARS (MAKE 2)

With Worsted weight yarn in tan, make a magic ring, ch 1.

Rnd 1: 5 sc in ring, pull ring closed tight (5 sts).

Rnd 2: 2 sc in each st around. Place marker for beginning of rnd and move marker up as each rnd is completed (10 sts).

Rnds 3-4: sc in each st around.

Fasten off.

Flatten ears. Sew ears slightly cupped to top of head.

LEGS (MAKE 2)

With Worsted weight yarn in tan, make a magic ring, ch 1.

Rnd 1: 6 sc in ring, pull ring closed tight (6 sts).

Rnd 2: 2 sc in each st around. Place marker for beginning of rnd and move marker up as each rnd is completed (12 sts).

Rnds 3-5: sc in each st around.

Rnd 6: *sc in next 2 sts, sc2tog* 3 times (9 sts).

Rnd 7: sc in each st around.

Sl st in next st. Fasten off.

Stuff legs. Set body on a flat surface and pin legs to front as pictured so that bear will sit nicely. Sew legs in place.

TAIL

With Worsted weight yarn in tan, make a magic ring, ch 1.

Rnd 1: 4 sc in ring, pull ring closed tight (4 sts).

Rnd 2: 2 sc in each st around. Place marker for beginning of rnd and move marker up as each rnd is completed (8 sts).

Rnd 3: sc in each st around.

Sl st in next st. Fasten off.

Set body on a flat surface and pin tail to back so that bear won't topple backwards. Sew tail in place, pushing in a bit of stuffing when a small gap remains.

ARMS (MAKE 2)

With Worsted weight yarn in tan, make a magic ring, ch 1.

Rnd 1: 6 sc in ring, pull ring closed tight (6 sts).

Rnd 2: *sc in next st, 2 sc in next st* 3 times) (9 sts)

Rnds 3-4: sc in each st around.

Rnd 5: *sc in next st, sc2tog* 3 times (6 sts)

Rnds 6-10: sc in each st around.

Sl st in next st. Fasten off. Stuff hand only; do not stuff arm.

Optional: At this point, pipe cleaners can be inserted in arms so that they will hold a pose. See Partial Armature, page 68.

Sew arms to sides of body as pictured.

SNOUT

With Worsted weight yarn in white, make a magic ring, ch 1.

Rnd 1: 6 sc in ring, pull ring closed tight (6 sts).

Rnd 2: 2 sc in each st around. Place marker for beginning of rnd and move marker up as each rnd is completed (12 sts).

Sl st in next st. Fasten off.

Sew bead to snout for nose. Sew snout to head with sewing thread.

VEST

Note: A chain 1 at the beginning of a row is for turning your work and does not count as a stitch.

With DK, Light Worsted yarn, loosely ch 26.

Row 1: ch 1, turn, sc in each st across (26 sts).

Row 2: ch 1, turn, sc in next 4 sts, loosely ch 5, skip 5 sts, sc in next 8 sts, loosely ch 5, skip 5 sts, sc in last 4 sts (16 sts, 10 chs).

Row 3: ch 1, turn, sc in each st or ch across (26 sts).

Rows 4-5: ch 1, turn, sc in each st across. Fasten off.

For 1st tie, ch 25; **to connect at neckline**, sl st in top 26 chs of vest; **for 2nd tie**, ch 25 (26 sts, 50 chs).

Fasten off. Pull knots tight at ends of ties, trim tails to 1/2".

Weave in ends.

Honey Ant

When you pinch Honey Ant's head, the mouth will move—and you're guaranteed to smile! I recommend putting pipe cleaners in the arms and legs (see Partial Armature, page 68). This will enable the limbs to hold a pose and help Honey Ant sit on the Picnic Blanket.

SIZE

7" tall, not including antennae

SUPPLIES

G6/4mm crochet hook
Small amount of Worsted weight yarn in rust and pink (ant)
Small amount of DK, Light Worsted yarn (skirt)
2 black safety eyes, 8-9mm
4 pipe cleaners in brown (optional)
Invisible sewing thread
Stuffing

MOUTH

With Worsted weight yarn in pink, make a magic ring, ch 1.

Rnd 1: 6 sc in ring, pull ring closed tight (6 sts).

Rnd 2: 2 sc in each st around (12 sts).

Rnd 3: *sc in next st, 2 sc in next st* 6 times (18 sts).

Rnd 4: *sc in next 2 sts, 2 sc in next st* 6 times (24 sts).
Fasten off. Weave in ends.

HEAD

With Worsted weight yarn in rust, make a magic ring, ch 1.

Rnd 1: 6 sc in ring, pull ring closed tight (6 sts).

Rnd 2: 2 sc in each st around. Place marker for beginning of rnd and move marker up as each rnd is completed (12 sts).

Rnd 3: *sc in next st, 2 sc in next st* 6 times (18 sts).

Rnd 4: *sc in next 5 sts, 2 sc in next st* 3 times (21 sts).

Rnd 5: *sc in next 6 sts, 2 sc in next st* 3 times (24 sts).

Rnd 6: sc in each st around.

Align edge of mouth with rim of head, wrong sides together.

Rnd 7: (see Photo A) to attach 1st half of mouth, work thru **head and mouth** with sc in next 12 sts;

A

now work in **head only** (see Photo B) and sc in next 12 sts (24 sts).

B

Rnd 8: (see Photo C) working in 2nd half of **mouth only**, sc in next 12 sts; working in **head only**, sc in next 12 sts (24 sts).

C

Rnd 9: (see Photo D) working in **back loops only**, *sc in next 2 sts, sc2tog* 3 times; resuming work in **both loops**, *sc in next 2 sts, sc2tog* 3 times (18 sts).

D

Rnd 10: (see Photo E) *sc in next st, sc2tog* 6 times (12 sts). Fasten off with long tail.

E

Attach eyes between Rnds 5-6 with an interspace of 6 sts; or eyes may be glued in later if desired. Stuff head carefully so that mouth stays concave by laying your thumb in mouth while you stuff: first stuff top of head, next stuff behind mouth, then stuff bottom (under mouth).

To secure mouth: With invisible sewing thread, make several stitches into crease of mouth and out through grooves between rnds in back of head.

BODY

With Worsted weight yarn in rust, make a magic ring, ch 1.

Rnd 1: 6 sc in ring, pull ring closed tight (6 sts).

Rnd 2: 2 sc in each st around (12 sts).

Rnd 3: *sc in next st, 2 sc in next st* 6 times (18 sts).

Rnd 4: *sc in next 2 sts, 2 sc in next st* 6 times (24 sts).

Rnds 5-7: sc in each st around.

Rnd 8: *sc in next 2 sts, sc2tog* 6 times (18 sts).

Rnd 9: sc in each st around.

Rnd 10: *sc in next st, sc2tog* 6 times (12 sts).

Rnd 11: *sc in next st, 2 sc in next st* 6 times (18 sts).

Rnds 12-14: sc in each st around.

Rnd 15: *sc in next st, sc2tog* 6 times (12 sts).

Sl st in next st. Fasten off.

Stuff body. Sew body to head. Weave in ends.

LEGS (MAKE 2)

With Worsted weight yarn in rust, make a magic ring, ch 1.

Rnd 1: 8 sc in ring, pull ring closed tight (8 sts).

Rnd 2: 2 sc in next st, sc in next st, 2 sc in next 3 sts, sc in next st, 2 sc in next 2 sts (14 sts).

Rnd 3: sc in each st around.

Rnd 4: sc in next 3 sts, sc2tog 4 times, sc in next 3 sts (10 sts).

Rnd 5: sc in next st, sc2tog 4 times, sc in next st (6 sts).

Rnds 6-15: sc in each st around.

Sl st in next st. Fasten off.

With eraser end of new pencil or long tweezers, stuff leg; stuff lightly near top of leg.

Sew legs to front of body on Rnds 3-4. Weave in ends.

Sew Legs to Front of Body on Rnds 3-4

Body Bottom

SKIRT

ARMS (MAKE 2)

With Worsted weight yarn in rust, make a magic ring, ch 1.

Rnd 1: 8 sc in ring, pull ring closed tight (8 sts).

Rnds 2-3: sc in each st around. Place marker for beginning of rnd and move marker up as each rnd is completed.

Rnd 4: sc2tog twice, sc in next 4 sts (6 sts).

Rnds 5-16: sc in each st around.

Sl st in next st. Fasten off. With eraser end of new pencil or long tweezers, push stuffing into hand only; do not stuff arm.

Sew an arm to each side of body. Weave in ends.

ANTENNAE (MAKE 2)

With Worsted weight yarn in rust, leave a long starting tail, ch 7. Sl st in 2nd ch from hook and in each remaining ch across: make sure to work your sl sts under the top loop and the back bump. Fasten off.

Use tails to sew antennae to head. Weave ends into head.

The skirt is a wraparound that ties in a bow at the back.

Note: A chain 1 at the beginning of a row is for turning your work and does not count as a stitch.

With DK, Light Worsted yarn, loosely ch 14.

Row 1: ch 1, turn, 2 dc in each st across (28 sts).

Row 2: ch 1, turn, 2 dc in each st across (56 sts).

Rows 3-6: ch 1, turn, dc in each st across.

Fasten off.

For 1st tie, ch 30; **to connect at waistline,** sc in top 14 chs of skirt; **for 2nd tie,** ch 30 (14 sts, 60 chs).

Fasten off. Pull knots tight at ends of ties, trim tails to 1/2".

Weave in ends.

Honey Bee

Honey Bee is lots of fun for play. Pinch the doll's head and its mouth will move! I recommend putting pipe cleaners in the arms and legs (see Partial Armature, page 68). This will enable the limbs to hold a pose and help Honey Bee sit on the picnic blanket.

SIZE

6" tall, not including antennae

SUPPLIES

G6/4mm crochet hook

Small amount of Worsted weight yarn in yellow, black & white

2 black safety eyes, 8-9mm

4 pipe cleaners in black (optional)

Invisible sewing thread

Stuffing

MOUTH

With black yarn, make a magic ring, ch 1.

Rnd 1: 6 sc in ring, pull ring closed tight (6 sts).

Rnd 2: 2 sc in each st around (12 sts).

Rnd 3: *sc in next st, 2 sc in next st* 6 times (18 sts).

Rnd 4: *sc in next 2 sts, 2 sc in next st* 6 times (24 sts).

Fasten off. Weave in ends.

HEAD

With yellow yarn, make a magic ring, ch 1.

Rnd 1: 6 sc in ring, pull ring closed tight (6 sts).

Rnd 2: 2 sc in each st around. Place marker for beginning of rnd and move marker up as each rnd is completed (12 sts).

Rnd 3: *sc in next st, 2 sc in next st* 6 times (18 sts).

Rnd 4: *sc in next 5 sts, 2 sc in next st* 3 times (21 sts).

Rnd 5: *sc in next 6 sts, 2 sc in next st* 3 times (24 sts).

Rnd 6: sc in each st around.

Align edge of mouth with rim of head, wrong sides together.

Rnd 7: (see Photo A, page 59) to attach 1st half of mouth, work thru **head and mouth** with sc in next 12 sts; now work in **head only** (see Photo B, page 59) and sc in next 12 sts (24 sts).

Rnd 8: (see Photo C, page 60) working in 2nd half of **mouth only**, sc in next 12 sts; working in **head only**, sc in next 12 sts (24 sts).

Rnd 9: (see Photo D, page 60) working in **back loops only**, *sc in next 2 sts, sc2tog* 3 times; resuming work in **both loops**, *sc in next 2 sts, sc2tog* 3 times (18 sts).

Rnd 10: (see Photo E, page 60) *sc in next st, sc2tog* 6 times (12 sts).

Fasten off with long tail.

Attach eyes between Rnds 5-6 with an interspace of 5 sts; or eyes may be glued in later if desired. Stuff head carefully so that mouth stays concave by laying your thumb in mouth while you stuff: first stuff top of head, next stuff behind mouth, then stuff bottom (under mouth).

To secure mouth: With invisible sewing thread, make several stitches into crease of mouth and out through grooves between rnds in back of head.

BODY

With yellow yarn, make a magic ring, ch 1.

Rnd 1: 6 sc in ring, pull ring closed tight (6 sts).

Rnd 2: 2 sc in each st around; change to black yarn in last st (12 sts).

Rnd 3: sl st loosely in first st, 2 sc in next st, *sc in next st, 2 sc in next st* 5 times (18 sts).

Rnd 4: *sc in next 2 sts, 2 sc in next st* 6 times; change to yellow yarn in last st (24 sts).

Rnd 5: sl st loosely in first st, sc in each remaining st around (24 sts).

Rnd 6: sc in each st around; change to black yarn in last st.

Rnd 7: sl st loosely in first st, sc in each remaining st around (24 sts).

Rnd 8: sc in each st around; change to yellow yarn in last st.

Rnd 9: sl st loosely in first st, sc in each remaining st around (24 sts).

Rnd 10: *sc in next 2 sts, sc2tog* 6 times; change to black yarn in last st (18 sts).

Rnd 11: sl st loosely in first st, sc in each remaining st around (18 sts).

Rnd 12: *sc in next st, sc2tog* 6 times (12 sts).

Sl st in next st. Fasten off.

Stuff body. Sew body to head with invisible thread.

LEGS (MAKE 2)

With black yarn, make a magic ring, ch 1.

Rnd 1: 8 sc in ring, pull ring closed tight (8 sts).

Rnd 2: 2 sc in next st, sc in next st, 2 sc in next 3 sts, sc in next st, 2 sc in next 2 sts (14 sts).

Rnd 3: sc in each st around.

Rnd 4: sc in next 3 sts, sc2tog 4 times, sc in next 3 sts (10 sts).

Rnd 5: sc in next st, sc2tog 4 times, sc in next st (6 sts).

Rnd 6-15: sc in each st around.

Sl st in next st. Fasten off.

With eraser end of new pencil or long tweezers, stuff leg; stuff lightly near top of leg.

Sew legs to front of body on Rnds 3-4. Weave in ends.

ARMS (MAKE 2)

With black yarn, make a magic ring, ch 1.

Rnd 1: 8 sc in ring, pull ring closed tight (8 sts).

Rnds 2-3: sc in each st around. Place marker for beginning of rnd and move marker up as each rnd is completed.

Rnd 4: sc2tog twice, sc in next 4 sts (6 sts).

Rnds 5-13: sc in each st around.

Sl st in next st. Fasten off. With eraser end of new pencil or long tweezers, push stuffing into hand only; do not stuff arm.

Sew an arm to each side of body. Weave in ends.

ANTENNAE (MAKE 2)

With black yarn, leave a long starting tail, ch 7.

Sl st in 2nd ch from hook and in each remaining ch across; make sure to work your sl sts under the top loop and the back bump. Fasten off.

Use tails to sew antennae to head. Weave ends into head.

WINGS (MAKE 2)

Note: A chain 1 at the beginning of a row is for turning your work and does not count as a stitch.

With white yarn, ch 2.

Row 1: 3 sc in 2nd ch from hook (3 sts).

Row 2: ch 1, turn, 2 sc in each st across (6 sts).

Row 3: ch 1, turn, 2 sc in each st across (12 sts).

Fasten off. Sew wings to back of body.

Stitches

SLIP KNOT

This is used to make a starting loop on the crochet hook.

1. Make a loop about 5 inches from end of yarn. Insert hook in loop and hook onto supply yarn (yarn coming from ball) at A.

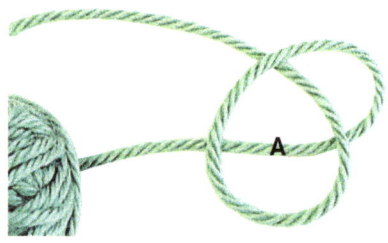

2. Pull yarn through loop.

3. Pull yarn ends to tighten loop around hook.

SLIP STITCH (SL ST)

1. Insert hook in stitch. Yarn over and pull through stitch and through loop on hook (A and B).

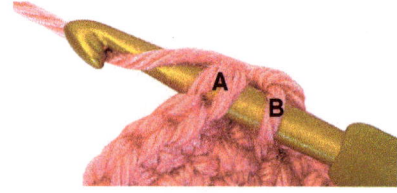

2. The sl st is done.

CHAIN (CH)

Start with a slip knot on hook.

1. Bring yarn **over** hook from back to front. Catch yarn with hook and pull it through the loop —

to look like this. One ch is done.

SINGLE CROCHET (SC)

This simple stitch is the primary stitch for amigurumi.

1. Insert hook in designated stitch. Note: Put hook under **both loops** that form v-shape at top of stitch unless otherwise instructed.

2. Yarn over and pull through the stitch (A).

You now have 2 loops on the hook:

3. Yarn over and pull through both loops on hook.

4. You now have 1 loop on hook and the sc stitch is done.

HALF DOUBLE CROCHET (HDC)

1. Yarn over and insert hook in designated stitch.

2. Yarn over and pull through the stitch (A).

You now have 3 loops on hook:

3. Yarn over and pull through all 3 loops on hook (A, B & C).

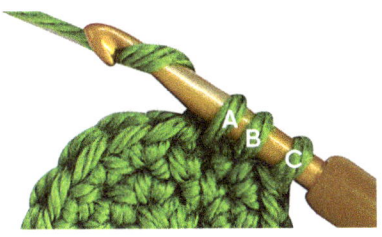

4. You now have 1 loop on hook and the hdc stitch is done.

DOUBLE CROCHET (DC)

1. Yarn over and insert hook in designated stitch.

2. Yarn over and pull through the stitch (A).

You now have 3 loops on hook:

3. Yarn over and pull through 1st 2 loops on hook (A and B).

You now have 2 loops on hook:

4. Yarn over and pull through both loops on hook.

5. You now have 1 loop on hook and the dc stitch is done.

SINGLE CROCHET 2 TOGETHER (SC2TOG)

This stitch is used to decrease 2 stitches into 1 stitch.

1. Insert hook in stitch, yarn over and pull up a loop — to look like this:

2. Insert hook in next stitch, yarn over and pull up a loop — to look like this:

3. Yarn over and pull through all 3 loops on hook — to look like this. The sc2tog is done.

SINGLE CROCHET 3 TOGETHER (SC3TOG)

This stitch is used to decrease 3 stitches into 1 stitch.

(Insert hook in next st and pull up a loop) **3 times**, yarn over and pull through all 4 loops on hook

DOUBLE CROCHET 2 TOGETHER (DC2TOG)

This stitch is used to decrease 2 stitches into 1 stitch.

1. Yarn over, insert hook in st and pull up a loop.

2. Yarn over and pull through 2 loops.

3. Yarn over, insert hook in next st and pull up a loop.

4. Yarn over, pull through 2 loops.

5. Yarn over and pull through all 3 loops on hook.

6. You now have 1 loop on your hook and the dc2tog is done.

Techniques

★ MAGIC RING

Most all of my amigurumi begins with the magic ring. This is an adjustable loop that makes a neat center when crocheting in the round. If you're not familiar with it, you may want to watch a YouTube tutorial. It's not difficult — and well worth it.

An alternative to the magic ring, if desired, is to ch 2; then begin Rnd 1 by working the required number of sts as stated in the pattern into the 2nd ch from the hook, This method will leave a small hole in the middle of the first round (see photo below).

Magic Ring

Ch 2

Make the Magic Ring as follows:

1. Make a ring a few inches from end of yarn. Grasp ring between thumb and index finger where the join makes an X. Insert hook in ring, hook onto supply yarn at Y and pull up a loop —

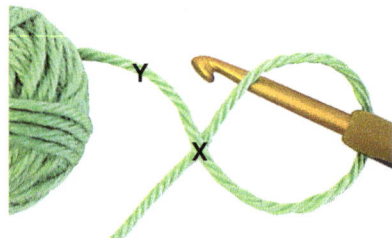

to look like this.

2. Chain 1 —

to look like this. This chain does not count as a stitch.

3. Insert hook into ring so you're crocheting over ring and yarn tail. Pull up a loop to begin your first single crochet —

and complete the single crochet.

4. Continue to crochet over ring and yarn tail for the specified number of single crochets for the 1st round.

5. Pull tail to close up ring. To begin the 2nd round, insert hook in 1st stitch of 1st round (see arrow).

BEGIN 2ND RND HERE

WORKING IN THE ROUND

Working in the round is crocheting in a continuous spiral. Lots of amigurumi is worked this way.

WORKING IN LOOPS

When a single crochet stitch is made, you will see 2 loops in a v-shape at the top of the stitch. To crochet the patterns in this book, insert your hook under **both loops** unless instructed otherwise. Crocheting in the "front loops only" or the "back loops only" is sometimes used for a different effect.

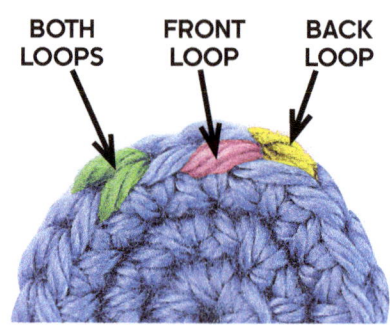
BOTH LOOPS FRONT LOOP BACK LOOP

CHANGING COLORS

To change color while single crocheting, work last stitch of old color to last yarn over, yarn over with new color and pull through both loops to complete the stitch.

ROTATING YOUR HOOK

When you wrap yarn over your hook, the front of the hook should be facing you. Then when it's time to pull the yarn through the loop on the hook, rotate the hook downward. It will slide easily through the loop instead of getting caught.

COUNTING ROUNDS

Periodically, it is good to count your rounds to ensure your place in a pattern. Fortunately, rounds are clearly defined and counting is easy. Each round makes a ridge. A groove separates the rounds. You need only to count the ridges. Take a look at the photo below to see that the circle has 5 rounds.

USING STITCH MARKERS

It can be tricky to keep track of your place when working in the round, so be sure to use a stitch marker. Place the stitch marker in the first stitch of a round — after completing the stitch. When you've crocheted all the way around, remove the stitch marker, make the next stitch, and replace the marker in the stitch just made. This will be the first stitch of the next round.

RUNNING STITCH MARKER

Stitch markers are essential in amigurumi to mark specific spots on your work. You can use one any time you feel it is necessary and sometimes the pattern will indicate that a marker is needed. A Running Stitch Marker is a scrap of yarn in a contrasting color that is woven back and forth between rounds. I especially like this type of marker for narrow cylinders such as arms and legs.

When you complete your first round, lay your "marker-yarn" over your work before starting the next round. Then when you work the first stitch of the next round, the yarn will be trapped between the stitches. At the end of each successive round, fold the marker-yarn back over your work: if it's in the back, fold it to the front, if it's in the front, fold it to the back. This way the yarn is flipped back and forth—between the last stitch of each round and the first stitch of the next round. When you're done, simply pull the marker-yarn out.

FASTENING OFF

This is the way to finish a piece so that it won't unravel. When you're done crocheting, cut the yarn and leave a tail. Wrap the tail over your hook and pull it all the way through the last loop left on your hook. Pull the tail tight and it will make a knot.

SMOOTHING THE EDGE

When fastening off, the knot can make a small bump in the edge of your work so that, for example, a round shape will not look as round as it should. To make the edge smooth, thread the long tail in a yarn needle and insert the needle down thru the center "V" of the next stitch.

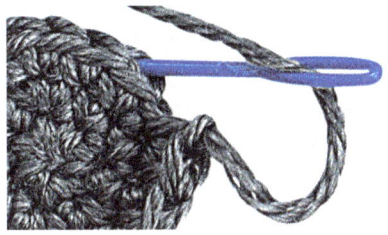

JOINING YARN

To join new yarn onto a crocheted item, such as to make a border, strap or sleeve, insert hook in desired stitch, make a loop and pull it through the stitch.

JOINING WITH SL ST

Start with a Slip Knot on hook. Insert hook in specified stitch. Yarn over and pull through the stitch and the loop on the hook.

JOINING WITH SC

Put yarn on hook with a Slip Knot. Insert hook in indicated stitch. Complete sc as shown in Single Crochet tutorial, page 64, steps 2-4.

ASSEMBLING

The assembly stage of amigurumi is an exciting time. This is when various pieces are sewn together and the project blossoms in cuteness! Thread a yarn needle with the tail of your auxiliary piece (arm, leg, etc.) and use a whip stitch or running stitch to sew it in place. You may want to pin your pieces in place beforehand to be sure the position looks good. A sewing needle and thread can also be used to sew your parts together. In some cases, this will make the stitches less visible.

WEAVING IN ENDS

The assembly of every pattern includes the instruction to weave in the ends. This is the way to hide and secure all of your straggly yarn tails. Thread the yarn end into a yarn needle, then skim through the back of the stitches on the wrong side of your work. Continue for about 2 inches, then turn and double back to lock the yarn into place. Trim the end close. When you turn your work to the right side, you should not see the woven ends. They should be tucked into the middle of your crocheted fabric.

FRENCH KNOT

Bring needle up from wrong side at A. Place needle close to fabric and wrap yarn around needle 2 or 3 times. Push needle down at a point near A.

A

ADDING WIRE

Optional armatures, or wire frameworks, can make amigurumi more dynamic by enabling a character to hold a pose. It can be placed in the arms, legs or both.

FULL ARMATURE

If your doll is made for display, not for play, this will make your doll more like an action figure than a cuddly stuffie. Use a heavy wire of 16 to 19 gauge. Begin when the doll's head/body are stuffed and connected and all parts are made.

Stuff hands & feet. The arms won't need stuffed. If legs are thick enough, you can add stuffing around wire after wire is inserted.

For the **arms**, lay doll down with arms outstretched in position and cut a piece of wire to that length plus 1/2 inch.

1. Bend one end into a small loop with needle-nose pliers and insert into first arm thru to hand.

2. Insert exposed end of wire into body where the arm will be placed.

3. Push wire all the way thru body to opposite side where you will sew the other arm.

4. Bend exposed tip of wire into a small loop and insert into 2nd arm.

5. Sew both arms to body around wire core.

For the **legs**, lay doll down with legs in position. Cut 2 pieces of wire long enough to extend from foot thru body into middle of head.

1. Bend one end into a small loop and insert into first leg thru to foot.

2. Insert exposed end of wire into body where the leg will be placed.

3. Push wire all the way thru body and into head.

4. Repeat for second leg.

5. Sew both legs to body around wire cores.

Tips: If you have trouble pushing the wire thru the stuffing, use a wooden skewer to make a tunnel. A wire armature can be secured in place by sewing into the hands and feet and working your needle thru the wire loop.

PARTIAL ARMATURE

Pipe Cleaners are great for creating arms and legs with some posability but more softness than a full armature. They are light, very flexible and they can be bent as often as you like. Begin when the doll's head/body are stuffed and connected and all parts are made.

Stuff hands and feet. The arms won't need stuffing. If the legs are thick enough, you can add stuffing around the pipe cleaner after it is inserted.

1. Bend pipe cleaner in half around a pen to make a U (see Photo A).

A

2. Make a small loop at the bend (see Photo B).

B

3. Twist the sides together (see Photo C).

C

Insert loop-first in limb so that loop goes down into the hand or foot. Cut off excess length.

Sew limb in place.

Note: If space permits, you can hold 2 pipe cleaners together and follow the instructions as usual. This will give the armature more strength and thickness.

Templates

PICNIC BASKET TEMPLATE

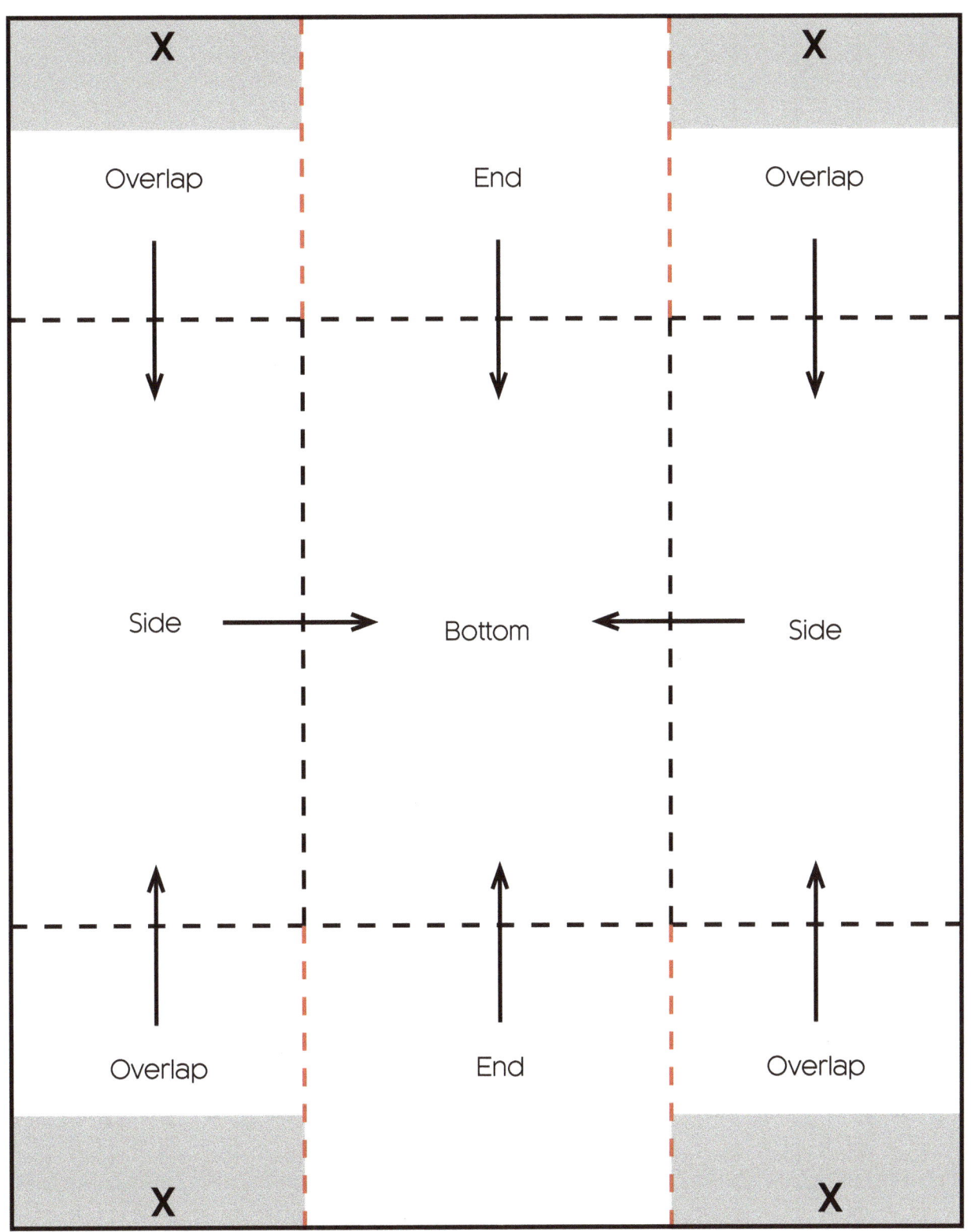

PICNIC BASKET LINING

Remove page from book or copy page on a color printer to use for your Picnic Basket's lining.

Resources

YARN

Amazon
amazon.com

Herrschners
herrschners.com

Joann Fabric and Craft Stores
joann.com

Lovecrafts
lovecrafts.com

NOTIONS

Amazon
amazon.com

Joann Fabric and Craft Stores
joann.com

SAFETY EYES

Amazon
amazon.com

CR's Crafts
crscrafts.com

Etsy Shop 6060
etsy.com/shop/6060

Glass Eyes Online
glasseyesonline.com

VIDEO TUTORIALS

youtube.com
Search on the name of the stitch or technique you want to learn.

pinterest.com/LindalooEnt/
Visit my Pinterest page to view video tutorials for the stitches and techniques used in this book. Look for the board named "Amigurumi Tutorials".

Yarn

The following yarns were used for these projects.

Honey Pie (Worsted, #4)
Lion Brand "Vanna's Choice", Beige
Lion Brand "Vanna's Choice", Pink
Lion Brand "Vanna's Choice", Honey

Wildflower Dress (DK, Light Worsted, #3)
Loops & Threads "Joy DK", Lavender
Lion Brand "Bonbons", Brights

Birdie Dress
Stylecraft "Special DK", Black
Stylecraft "Special DK", White
Sirdar "Happy Cotton", Freckle
Sirdar "Happy Cotton", Juicy
Sirdar "Happy Cotton", Buttercup

Basic Blouse (DK, Light Worsted, #3)
Stylecraft "Special DK", Boysenberry
Willow Yarns "Daily DK", Campfire

Daisy Top (DK, Light Worsted, #3)
Bergere de France "Barisienne", Marron
Bergere de France "Barisienne", Boutonor
Bergere de France "Barisienne", Clapotis
Bergere de France "Barisienne", Methylene

Jacket (DK, Light Worsted, #3)
Stylecraft "Special DK", Lime

Honey Bear Blouse (DK, Light Worsted, #3)
Stylecraft "Special DK", Meadow
Stylecraft "Special DK", Camel
Stylecraft "Special DK", Cream

Drawstring Shorts (DK, Light Worsted, #3)
Stylecraft "Special DK", Bottle
Stylecraft "Special DK", Camel

Butterfly Jeans (DK, Light Worsted, #3)
Stylecraft "Special DK", Denim

Fancy Pants (DK, Light Worsted, #3)
Red Heart "Fashion Soft", Atlantis
Stylecraft "Special DK", Lime

Button-Front Skirt (DK, Light Worsted, #3)
Stylecraft "Special DK", Walnut

Simple Skirt (DK, Light Worsted, #3)
  Bergere de France "Barisienne", Clapotis

Espadrilles (DK, Light Worsted, #3)
  Stylecraft "Special DK", Camel
  Loops & Threads "Joy DK", Iris

Ballet Flats (DK, Light Worsted, #3)
  Stylecraft "Special DK", Tomato

Sandals (DK, Light Worsted, #3)
  Stylecraft "Special DK", Walnut

Bow Barrette (DK, Light Worsted, #3)
  Red Heart "Baby Hugs Light", Lilac

Flower Barrette (DK, Light Worsted, #3)
  Loops & Threads "Joy DK", Blossom

Watermelon Purse (DK, Light Worsted, #3)
  Red Heart "Baby Hugs Light", Peachie
  Red Heart "Baby Hugs Light", Shell
  Herrschners "Kids' Brites", Grasshopper
  Red Heart "Fashion Soft", Black

Tote Bag (Worsted, #4)
  Red Heart "Soft", Turquoise
  Red Heart "Soft", Lemon

Barbecue Apron (DK, Light Worsted, #3)
  Loops & Threads "Snuggly Wuggly", Candy Pink
  Red Heart "Baby Hugs Light", Lilac

Nightgown (DK, Light Worsted, #3)
  Loops & Threads "Joy DK", Summit
  Loops & Threads "Joy DK", Blossom

Slice-of-Pie Sleeping Bag (Worsted, #4)
  Red Heart "Soft", Honey
  Red Heart "Soft", Off White

Picnic Blanket (Worsted, #4)
  Caron "Simply Soft", Raspberry or Autumn Red
  Caron "Simply Soft", Strawberry
  Caron "Simply Soft", Off-White

Barbecue Pit Play Mat (Worsted, #4)
  Caron "Simply Soft", Black
  (DK, Light Worsted, #3)
  Hobby Lobby "I Love This Yarn", Red
  Hobby Lobby "I Love This Yarn", Orange

Picnic Basket (Worsted, #4)
  Red Heart "Soft", Cocoa

Cheeseburger (DK, Light Worsted, #3)
  Stylecraft "Special DK", Camel
  Stylecraft "Special DK", Walnut
  Red Heart "Baby Hugs Light", Sunny
  Premier "Primo", Red
  Lion Brand "Baby Soft", Pistachio

Chicken Drumstick (DK, Light Worsted, #3)
  Red Heart "Fashion Soft", Flax
  Lion Brand "Vanna's Style", Camel

Corn on the Cob (DK, Light Worsted, #3)
  Red Heart "Baby Hugs Light", Sunny
  Premier "Deborah Norville Everyday Baby", Green

Watermelon (DK, Light Worsted, #3)
  Red Heart "Baby Hugs Light", Peachie
  Red Heart "Baby Hugs Light", Shell
  Herrschners "Kids' Brites", Grasshopper
  Red Heart "Fashion Soft", Black

Fruit Drink (DK, Light Worsted, #3)
- Loops & Threads "Joy DK", Lavender
- Loops & Threads "Joy DK", Iris
- Loops & Threads "Joy DK", Summit
- Premier "Primo", Cream
- Baby Bee "Sweet Delight", Tangerine
- Red Heart "Baby Hugs Light", Orangie
- Premier "Deborah Norville Everyday Baby", Green
- Red Heart "Fashion Soft", Kelly Green

S'Mores (Worsted, #4)
- Lion Brand "Vanna's Choice", Honey
- (DK, Light Worsted, #3)
- Stylecraft "Special DK", Walnut
- Stylecraft "Special DK", White

Blueberry Pie (Worsted, #4)
- Caron "Simply Soft", Gray Heather
- Caron "Simply Soft", White
- (DK, Light Worsted, #3)
- Stylecraft "Special DK", Camel
- Bergere de France "Barisienne", Methylene

Ketchup & Mustard (DK, Light Worsted, #3)
- Bergere de France "Barisienne", Vitelotte
- Bergere de France "Barisienne", Boutonor

Potato Chips (DK, Light Worsted, #3)
- Red Heart "Baby Hugs Light", Sunny
- Red Heart "Baby Hugs Light", Shell
- Stylecraft "Special DK", Saffron

Hot Dog (DK, Light Worsted, #3)
- Stylecraft "Special DK", Raspberry
- Stylecraft "Special DK", Camel
- Bergere de France "Barisienne", Vitelotte
- Bergere de France "Barisienne", Boutonor

Vegetable Kebab (DK, Light Worsted, #3)
- Lion Brand "Baby Soft", Sweet Pea
- Stylecraft "Special DK", Bottle
- Stylecraft "Special DK", Lipstick
- Stylecraft "Special DK", Saffron
- Stylecraft "Special DK", Boysenberry
- Stylecraft "Special DK", White

Spatula
- Caron "SimplySoft", Chocolate
- Caron "Simply Soft", Grey Heather

Picnic Plates (Worsted, #4)
- Loops & Threads "Impeccable", Aqua
- Loops & Threads "Impeccable", Fern
- Loops & Threads "Impeccable", Lavender
- Loops & Threads "Impeccable", Pumpkin

Mini FrizzBee (Worsted, #4)
- Caron "Simply Soft", Sunshine
- Caron "Simply Soft", Black

Honey Bear (Worsted, #4)
- Red Heart "Soft", Wheat
- Red Heart "Soft", White
- (DK, Light Worsted, #3)
- Loops & Threads "Joy DK", Summit

Honey Ant (Worsted, #4)
- Lion Brand "Vanna's Choice", Rust
- Lion Brand "Vanna's Choice", Raspberry or Pink
- (DK, Light Worsted, #3)
- Loops & Threads "Joy DK", Iris

Honey Bee (Worsted, #4)
- Caron "Simply Soft", Sunshine
- Caron "Simply Soft", Black
- Caron "Simply Soft", White

Extras...just for fun!

Enjoy a
Honey Pie Coloring Page
and
Honey Pie Recipe.

Honey Pie Recipe

Choose a tasty honey for this fluffy no-bake pie with homemade whipped cream. I like Nature Nate's. This recipe makes a big pie, so be sure to get the large size of graham cracker crust.

1 10-inch ready-made graham cracker pie crust
2 3/4 cups heavy cream
2/3 cup honey, divided
8 ounces cream cheese, softened
1 package of instant vanilla pudding (5.1 ounce)
1 3/4 cups whole milk

1. Pour heavy cream in bowl of electric mixer. Add 1/3 cup honey and beat on high until whipped to firm peaks. Spoon whipped cream out of mixing bowl and refrigerate until ready to use.

2. Place cream cheese and remaining 1/3 cup honey in mixing bowl. Beat on high to soften the cream cheese. Reduce speed to low and alternate adding instant pudding powder and milk until ingredients are well-combined and smooth.

3. Spoon half of whipped cream into pudding mixture. Gently fold it in with a spatula until the mixture is light and even.

4. Spoon filling into pie crust and spread out evenly.

5. Mound remaining whipped cream on top and spread it over the surface, but not all the way to the edge.

Chill at least 4 hours before serving.

Other Books by Linda Wright

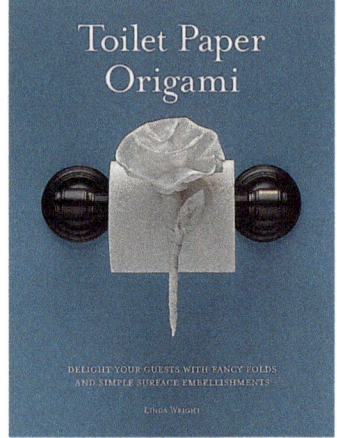

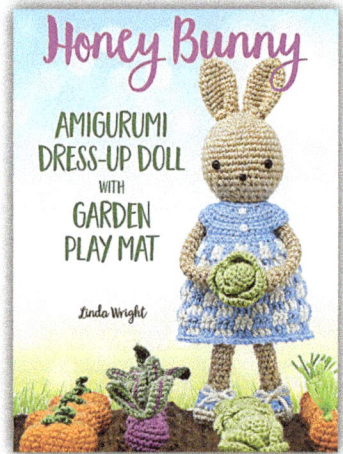

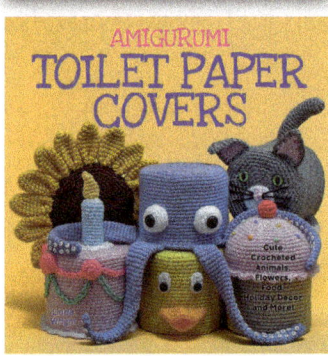
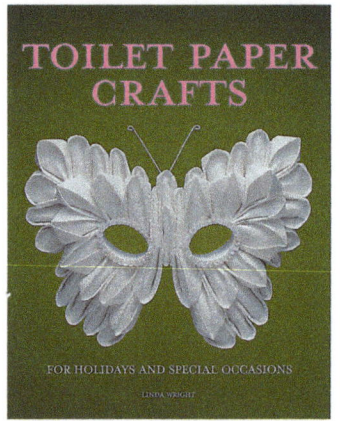
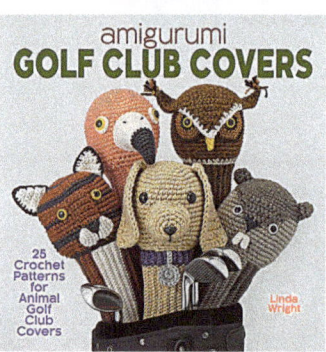
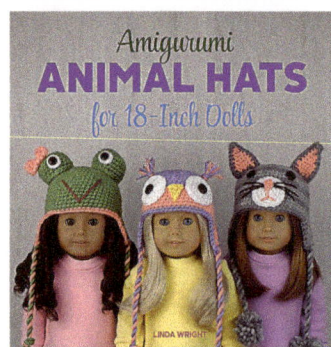

LINDA WRIGHT studied textiles, patternmaking and clothing design at the Pennsylvania State University and has had a lifelong love of creating. She is the author of various handicraft books including the groundbreaking *Toilet Paper Origami* and its companion book, *Toilet Paper Origami On a Roll*, as well as a collection of adult coloring books and numerous works of amigurumi-style crochet. To learn more about these fun-filled books, visit:

amazon.com/author/lindawright   pinterest.com/LindalooEnt   lindaloo.com

www.ingramcontent.com/pod-product-compliance
Lightning Source LLC
Chambersburg PA
CBHW061118170426
43199CB00026B/2955